A Belief
in Providence

Photo from an 1855 daguerreotype of Mother Theodore Guérin

INDIANA HISTORICAL SOCIETY PRESS
INDIANAPOLIS 2007

A Belief in Providence

A Life of Saint Theodora Guérin

JULIE YOUNG

Printed in the United States.

This book is a publication of the
Indiana Historical Society Press
450 West Ohio Street
Indianapolis, Indiana 46202-3269 USA

www.indianahistory.org

Telephone orders 1-800-447-1830
Fax orders 1-317-234-0562
Online orders @ shop.indianahistory.org

The paper in this publication meets the minimum requirements of American National Standard for information Sciences—Permanence of Paper for Printed Library Materials, ANSI Z39.48-1984.

Library of Congress Cataloging-in-Publication Data

Young, Julie.
  A belief in providence : a life of Saint Theodora Guérin / Julie Young.
    p, cm.
  Includes bibliographical references and index.
  ISBN 978-0-87195-255-4 (alk. paper)
    1. Guérin, Theodore, Saint, 1798-1856. 2. Sisters of Providence (Saint
Mary-of-the-Woods, Ind.)—Biography. 3. Nuns—United States—Biography. I. Title.
  BX4705.G65Y68 2007
  282.092—dc22

                                                        2006049723

A publication from the Eli Lilly Indiana History Book Fund

"Mother Theodore was a timely gift from God to renew the Church in its infancy in Indiana."

—*Most Reverend Daniel M. Buechlein, OSB*
Archbishop of Indianapolis

A Belief in Providence: A Life of Saint Theodora Guérin is made possible by a generous grant from Jerry and Rosie Semler and the Semler Family Foundation.

For my dad,
"Sail on Silver Girl . . ."

"What have we to do in order to become saints?
Nothing extraordinary; nothing more than we do every day.
Only do it for his love."
—*Saint Theodora Guérin*

Contents

Foreword

One hundred ninety years after Indiana became the nineteenth state of the United States of America a unique privilege was accorded one of the state's early pioneers and educators. On October 15, 2006, Mother Theodore Guérin was declared a saint by Pope Benedict XVI, becoming the first resident from Indiana to receive this title. Mother Theodore, the former Anne-Thérèse Guérin, came to Indiana from France in 1840 to establish the American foundation of the Sisters of Providence of Saint Mary-of-the-Woods. She came to continue the work in which she had been engaged in France for the previous seventeen years. In 1841, less than one year after her arrival in Indiana with five other French sisters, she opened Saint Mary's Female Institute, the forerunner of Saint Mary-of-the-Woods College, which today is the oldest Catholic liberal arts college in the United States. She opened schools in far-flung parts of the state—ten in all, in just sixteen years, accomplishing this feat in a period of time long before automobiles or interstate highways! Yet, her words and many works of love, mercy, and justice touched the lives of hundreds of people.

In the following pages the reader will discover a woman of great courage, vision, and wisdom. The title of this book, *A Belief in Providence*, is well chosen. Had Saint Mother Theodore believed only in her own or in others' human vision, wisdom, and loving care her courage would have run out long before her mission was accomplished. As it was, she placed all her trust in God. What she did to educate the young and to care for the poor and sick, she did because of her great love for God and for all of God's people of whatever race or creed.

From time to time, the Catholic Church raises up for our imitation and veneration those whose lives have exhibited a heroic degree of Christian virtue. This is not done lightly or without lengthy research, examination of records, and the hearing of personal testimonies. Finally, two examples of divine intervention in the laws of nature, which take place after a person or persons have asked for the intercession of God through the prayer of the holy person whose life is under examination, are required. You will learn much about Indiana's first solemnly proclaimed saint as you read these pages.

Sister Marie Kevin Tighe, SP
Saint Mary-of-the-Woods
January 2007

Acknowledgments

When I was little, I used to watch award shows, read books and album liner notes amazed at how many people a performer or author had to thank in their acknowledgments. I couldn't believe the lists these people had prepared, but now I realize just how many people make any one project possible. Now that I have realized my dream of becoming a published author, I too have a lot of people to thank for helping me along the way.

First and foremost, I would like to thank the Indiana Historical Society Press for having confidence in this project and considering it for publication. I want to thank Rachel Popma, Kathleen Breen, and Paula Corpuz for working with me in order to help this book come to fruition. You have truly been a dream to work with, and I really appreciate your support.

Words cannot describe the love and support I have received from Sister Marie Kevin Tighe, Sister Mary Ryan and the archives staff, and the Sisters of Providence and the Saint Mary-of-the-Woods College community. My gratitude is in every word I write. I am so blessed to be a "Woodsie."

I also want to thank Nancy Wilson of Heart and Oprah Winfrey whose kind words of encouragement taught me that anything really is possible and that when you reach one goal, it must be replaced with a new one. Without the two of you, this book would never have been written.

To my former teachers whose faith in me never wavered: thank you for having confidence in me. Kent Jackson, Mary Helen Eckrich, Helen Dalton, and Judy Nichols. I hope I have made you proud. Connie and Lena, thank you for being the best mentors anyone could have.

To my family: Shawn, you have gone above and beyond what anyone could expect in supporting this project and I appreciate it. Vincent, thank you for keeping things in perspective telling me, "You're not famous, just Catholic." Christopher, you are my inspiration and role model. Thank you for spreading your wings and showing me that I too could fly.

To my mom, I wouldn't have the faith I have without you. Your Catholic legacy is one I will carry with me forever. Thank you for everything.

Saint Theodora banner, Saint Peter's Square

Chapter I

Blessed among Women

Early in the morning of October 15, 2006, bleary-eyed pilgrims made their way to the gates of Saint Peter's Square in Vatican City, bundled against the chill in order to be first in line to bear witness to one of the biggest events in the Roman Catholic Church—the canonization of a saint. Those who made the journey from all parts of the globe wore colorful scarves, T-shirts, and pins bearing the names and images of the four saints that were to be honored. Some carried banners, while others carried their national flags or sang songs to pass the time. Among the handmade posters was a sign that read "Saint Theodora Guérin Rocks!" as well as a giant banner from Guerin Catholic High School in

Noblesville, Indiana. When the doors finally opened, the sea of humanity flooded the square, each person vying for the best seat from which to watch Pope Benedict XVI process into the square accompanied by a number of bishops from around the world and begin the canonization rite.

Unlike other lifetime achievement awards, a canonization, which celebrates the life lived by the candidate, takes place after the honoree's death, and though they are not present to hear the bells ringing, the choirs singing, or the words spoken for them, every person in attendance can feel their presence. Large banners hang from four of the five balconies of Saint Peter's Basilica, each one bearing a saint's likeness, and as each name is announced, the cheering that follows from their supporters resembles the sound at a rock concert. The Mass itself was in Latin, but Benedict XVI read his statement about each saint in his or her native language. (Although born in France, Saint Theodora was canonized as an American saint, and the pope read her biography in English.)

For some saints, the journey is longer than others. The Cause for Canonization is a slow and exact process that examines every aspect of a person's life. By the time a canonization ceremony occurs, hundreds and thousands of lives are invested in the moment when the pope listens to his or her biography and declares the candidate now and forever to be a role model for all Catholics. For those pilgrims who have traveled to watch history unfold, the event is the trip of a lifetime and the culmination of a lot of hard work. Among the attendees honoring the four who were to be canonized was a large delegation from the United States, Asia, and France who have waited nearly a century for the moment when the woman they consider to be their mother and sister would be counted among the elite group of Catholic saints to live their lives predominately in the United States and the first to be honored from the state of Indiana.

Long before women marched for equal rights and Title IX sought to change the way everyone looked at college and high school athletics; before Rosa Parks refused to give up her seat on a bus in Montgomery, Alabama, and Eleanor Roosevelt championed the plight of the common man; before Madam C. J. Walker became an entrepreneur and Susan B. Anthony campaigned for woman suffrage, there were women who helped settle the frontier and contributed to the growth of a young nation. One such woman was Mother Theodore Guérin, the foundress of the Sisters of Providence at Saint Mary-of-the-Woods.

Saint Mary-of-the-Woods is a small village just west of Terre Haute, Indiana, and is adjacent to Saint Mary-of-the-Woods College. Founded in 1840, "The Woods" is the oldest Catholic women's liberal arts college in the country, and thousands of women owe their education to the sisters who came to the Indiana wilderness armed only with the belief that Providence would see them through it. The Celtic cross in the Sisters of Providence cemetery that stands as a monument to Guérin's legacy bears the inscription, "I sleep, but my heart watches over this house which I have built." Each

Celtic cross, Saint Mary-of-the-Woods

day "Woods" women feel connected to the vision of Guérin, who broke through barriers more than 160 years ago to push forward the education of young women. She serves as a role model to those who live her legacy through their studies and through the belief that all things are possible with a reliance on God. Today, students carry out Guérin's spirit of love and generosity in more careers and vocations than she could have dreamed of when she first stepped onto Hoosier soil in 1840.

Hers is not the story of a fairy godmother who came to the vast Midwest, established a new community, and lived happily ever after. This is the story of a woman who was courageous enough to leave behind the only home she knew in order to devote herself to the education of youth in an untamed land. Although there had been a French presence in Indiana dating back to 1534 with Jacques Cartier's expedition, Guérin knew she would be despised by some even as she was welcomed by others. Many attempts by French missionaries to convert Native American tribes, such as the Kickapoo, Miami, Wea, and Piankeshaw, had failed. She knew she would meet people from a variety of cultures, as many new settlers were arriving in the Diocese of Vincennes, and it would be her job to merge those cultures into a working unit.

Indiana in the 1840s was not a choice duty station for any-one, but especially not a middle-aged, ailing Catholic sister who knew that her chances of returning to her beloved France were slim to none. Going to America was something akin to traveling to another planet. After all, there was a better-than-average chance that her journey would be futile and that her mission would fail. She had no script and very little guidance other than the Rule of the order, composed in 1835, stating that the sisters were to devote "themselves to the instruction of young girls and to the care of the unfortunate" in their homes, in hospitals, or in prisons. Most of her superiors in France had no idea just how big the Midwest was, and they could offer little to the new establishment other than moral support. Few, if any, had been in her position, and there was no way to fully describe what life in Indiana was like.

Still, she soldiered on, with the spirit of a true pioneer who was committed to the idea of ministering to the needs of homesteaders who were settling in the "raw, new state" of Indiana, which had no schools and few churches. Guérin made acquaintances in every town she stopped in along the way, forging lifelong relationships with people in New York, Baltimore, and Philadelphia. She and her companions welcomed the support she received from the kind strangers they met. Once arrived in Indiana, Guérin used her wit and head for business to anticipate the needs of not only her congregation, but also of the settlers who needed her as much as she needed them. She eventually befriended those who had shunned her and expanded her ministry throughout the state.

Freshmen registration, Saint Mary-of-the-Woods, 1946

Pope John Paul II described Guérin as "a woman of our time." Like many of today's women, she knew what it felt like to be held back from pursuing her calling to its highest level. Long before anyone knew what a "glass ceiling" was, she experienced the effects of it firsthand. Guérin was thwarted by men who could not stand to see her thrive and forced to watch helplessly while Celestine de la Hailandière, the bishop of Vincennes, interfered with her work, yet she did not indulge in self-pity or resentment. Her talent and drive earned her the respect of both friends and foes. Like many "mothers," she learned how to provide for the needs of many with only a handful of resources. She learned to make do and make the best of her situation, often relying on ingenuity. Yet, as John Paul II noted, "While she possessed all the gifts necessary for leadership and used them brilliantly, she was always humble and gave God all the credit for all the good she did."

Not only did Guérin know how to make a good business deal, she also was a prolific writer, journaling her experiences and creating what is the closest thing to an autobiography the world will ever have. Although she battled with her superior in Indiana, she was professional in her dealings, preferring not to "sling mud" or air dirty laundry, outlining grievances subtly in her letters rather than as a blatant cry for help. Luckily, Guérin was also blessed with a wry sense of humor that saw her through many difficult times. Above all, she had tremendous faith in God, who had led her to America and always seemed to provide when there was a need. She was quoted as saying, "We must put our faith in Providence which so far has never abandoned us."

Her faith saw her through the darkest times. "Her trust in her provident God was ever present in her life," said John Paul II. "She called upon God's providence in all things. . . . She recognized that all she did was in God's loving care." As a child in the years after the French Revolution, when many religious were forced into hiding in order to escape execution, Guérin probably knew of priests who fled Europe for the safety of America and was aware of some priests who only celebrated the sacraments in secrecy. This knowledge of prejudice aided her in overcoming the prejudices that she faced in America.

Many settlers were not enthusiastic about her arrival, and her congregation in Indiana was the victim of religious, gender, and cultural prejudice during the early years of her ministry. At one time, people even spat on the sisters. Eventually their hearts softened, and they allowed their children to be educated by the women. Guérin helped establish not only a network of friends within the Catholic establishments around the state, but also helped create a community that stood by her in her darkest hour.

Guérin's disagreements with Bishop Hailandière were ongoing throughout his tenure as the bishop of Vincennes. The two were often at odds because of monetary and ideological issues. Although Guérin tried to work with the bishop, she had her obligation to the Rule, which often conflicted with the bishop's way of doing things. It is doubtful, however, that the bishop was prepared to share any amount of power with anyone, much less a woman, and it is clear that he found running a huge diocese too much to handle. Guérin knew he was a difficult man, but she respected his authority and tried to work with him for the good of the common community. "Her love embraced even those who caused her pain and anguish," John Paul II said of Guérin.

Guérin's legacy lives on in the ministries of the Sisters of Providence. The Sisters of Providence continue to search for new avenues to improve the standard of life for women, the poor, and the sick. Through the establishment of schools and institutions, the order maintains a strong presence in ministries throughout the United States, China, and Taiwan. But the sisters are not the only ones dedicated to Guérin's mission. Catholic schools in the Midwest are establishing their connection to this remarkable woman with the naming of high schools in Indiana and Illinois. The Archdiocese of Indianapolis also bestows the Mother Theodore Guérin Award annually to educators who exemplify her values and virtue.

Although Guérin's life and legacy certainly indicated that hers was a life to be examined, it was not until 1909 when the formal informative process began. The first step toward beatification and canonization occurred when it was discovered that Guérin's brain had not decomposed as it should have in death. Bishop Francis Silas Chatard, who was also a physician, immediately assembled a team of doctors to consider Guérin's body. This initial phase lasted until 1913 and included testimony from twenty-four individuals who had encountered her or had firsthand accounts of her through others.

The healing of Sister Theodosia Mug ultimately led to Guérin's beatification. In 1908 Sister Theodosia was cured of numerous health issues and left an account of this event for posterity. According to her writings, she had been praying for another sister at Guérin's crypt. The following morning she reported that she was able to use her arm, which had been crippled for years. Sister Theodosia lived to be eighty-two years old and never had another episode of that particular affliction. In 1997 the healing was approved and declared a miracle, clearing the way for Guérin's beatification in 1998 where she was bestowed the title "Blessed."

In June 2005 a second miracle, which had been under investigation since 2003, passed medical scrutiny. Once again, the circumstances surrounded someone within the Saint Mary-of-the-Woods community. Phil McCord, who worked for the Sisters of Providence, was afflicted with an eye condition and was preparing for a surgery that he was very ambivalent about and asked Guérin to help in any way that she could. The next morning his condition seemed to be improved. Eventually, his physician said that he

Novices' chapel, Saint Mary-of-the-Woods, 1937

no longer needed the surgery. Sister Ann Margaret O'Hara, general superior of the congregation, addressed the significance of McCord's healing, stating, "It speaks volumes that a non-Catholic had enough faith to pray for this miracle and then to report it."

In November 2005, just months after the medical commission unanimously declared that there was no medical explanation for McCord's healing, the sisters received word that a seven-person theological commission appointed by the Vatican's Congregation for the Causes of Saints had approved Guérin's Cause. By February of 2006, the Ordinary Congregation of the Cardinals in Rome declared the second case a miracle, opening the way for Guérin's canonization. Information about the Cause was shared with a variety of church officials, including bishops and cardinals, before it was sent to Benedict XVI for approval. After receiving the news about the vote, Sister Ann Margaret informed the congregation. "It was just so moving to share this, and to know the reality of this woman and to know that her power is here, that power that she knows through the Spirit of God. . . . It calls me and it calls us as sisters of Providence to really live as she lived, to become more humble, more trusting in Providence, to serve people better, to give ourselves totally to this mission," Sister Ann Margaret said.

Mother Theodore Guérin's life and story are certainly worthy of a place as a role model in the history of the Catholic Church and as a pioneer in the history of Indiana. This volume revisits the journey of the slight French sister who cast her lot with Providence and whose ministry mushroomed in the decades that followed. Her perseverance is a lesson for many in the twenty-first century. Her story is truly a blueprint for our own.

Sister Ann Margaret O'Hara

11

Portrait of Mother Theodore commissioned by Bishop Jacques M. Maurice Landes d' Aussac de Saint-Palais

Chapter 2

Maternal Instincts

By 1798 the French region of Brittany, like many other regions of the nation, was still suffering from the effects of the French Revolution. Tired of the tax exemptions granted to the royal family and aristocracy, the people (middle class and peasants) of France sought to improve their position in life by forming the National Assembly on June 17, 1789. As many of the people continued to be disgruntled by the inconsistent treatment of the classes, the conflict exploded on July 14, 1789, when a crowd stormed the Bastille prison in Paris and freed a handful of prisoners inside. Revolutionaries not only captured and detained King Louis XVI, but he was also put to death by the guillotine on January 21, 1793.

His wife, Marie Antoinette, was killed in the same manner on October 16 of that same year.

In the chaos and terror that followed, a number of coups were staged at the hands of antirevolutionary and prorevolutionary groups. It is believed that between 18,500 and 40,000 people died during this time and that the guillotine was used more during the Reign of Terror (1793–94) than in any other time in French history.

Families who at one time had enjoyed a comfortable lifestyle were reduced to living on necessities. People of a noble lineage hid any and all reference to rank and station in order to survive. During the years of revolution the Catholic clergy of France was all but destroyed. Many members of the clergy were killed, while others went underground and were kept safe by loyal parishioners, who if caught hiding the religious were in danger of being executed. Some went into exile, while others looked for the chance to spread the gospel in other parts of the world.

In 1795 a power came to the forefront of France known as the Directory and included five members who were elected by the Council of Ancients and the Council of Five Hundred. Due to internal fighting, two members of the Directory, Paul Barras and Abbe (Emmanuel Joseph) Sieyès, worked with Napoléon Bonaparte, a young man who proved to be a military powerhouse during the revolution, to overthrow the other members in the Coup of Brumaire and form the Consulate. It would not be long before Napoléon himself would edge out the other two in order to rule the French Republic (1799–1804) and later as emperor of France (1804–1814).

As the conflict came to a close, twenty-six-year-old Laurent Guérin and twenty-five-year-old Isabelle Leferve were married in a small civil ceremony while Laurent was on leave from the navy. During the simple ceremony, attended by Laurent's older brother

Jean Baptist and friends Jean-Marie Hingant, Pierre Huertel, and Julien Joubin, the clerk read the birth certificates of the young citizens of the new republic as well as the banns that had been posted earlier. The republic ratified the marriage, and as the couple pledged their troth, they also pledged their union to God. Because religious services had not yet been restored, the couple kept its religious bond private.

It was into this uncertain world that Anne-Thérèse Guérin was born on October 2, 1798, in the small village of Etables. Members of her mother's family were staunch royalists of a lesser nobility, and many had died during the revolution. The only proof of Isabelle's former station was in a little cap that ladies of rank wore. Laurent's family had origins in Italy, and it is believed that his family supported Napoléon's regime.

The couple was quiet about its class, and despite the dangers all around them, gentility and grace were the foundation of the Guérin home. The family also balanced duties to church and state. The day after Anne-Thérèse's birth, Laurent and Isabelle registered her birth with the town and then had her secretly baptized at home, dedicating her life to the Virgin Mary. Despite the difficulties, the family made religion the cornerstone of its household.

By all accounts, Anne-Thérèse's childhood was a happy one. She was a lively, precocious, and mischievous child who had a fascination with the sea. Throughout her childhood and until she left home for the convent, she spent hours praying as she climbed the rocky shoreline near her home and walked along the quiet beach. She was also very obedient to her parents and worked hard to serve God. However, there were also sad times. Both of her brothers, Jean-Laurent and Laurent-Marie, died young; one of them burned to death when he slept too close to a fire. Only Anne-Thérèse and her sister Marie-Jeanne lived to adulthood.

Laurent's career as an officer in Napoléon's navy kept him away from home much of the time. As a typical military wife, Isabelle was the head of the household during his absences. Many public schools were still closed because of the war, and Isabelle educated her children at home, teaching them to read and designing lessons that focused largely on Christian values. Anne-Thérèse eventually attended school in Etables when she was nine, but she finished her formal education at home when a relative, who was a seminarian, moved into the family's home for a period of time.

Like many who receive the call to the religious life, Anne-Thérèse knew at a young age that she wanted to devote her life to serving God. She was so advanced in her religious instruction that she was permitted to receive her first communion at the age of ten, a full two years earlier than what was customary at the time. She later said that it was on that day that she gave herself to God, promising him that she would serve him when she was older. Though her prayer was not a binding vow, she took it very seriously even though she did not know what God's plan was for her.

Sadly, the world Anne-Thérèse knew and the life she was preparing for came to a grinding halt at the age of fifteen, when she learned of her beloved father's death. Laurent was returning from France after the defeat of the Russian emperor and had landed in the south of France for some hard-earned time off. During his journey home to see his wife and daughters, he was attacked and murdered by a group of bandits. Isabelle, devastated by the news of her husband's death, sank into a deep depression that lasted for ten years. She had lost countless family members at sea as well as two young sons. Another loss was inconceivable.

An equally devastated Anne-Thérèse had to deal with her mother's depression and the financial consequences of her father's death. She became the head of the household, tending the gardens and working as a seamstress to earn money to keep the family afloat.

Luckily, she had inherited her father's sharp business sense, making whatever deal she could to help her mother and sister survive. This keen sense of business served her well later in life.

As the sole provider for her family, Anne-Thérèse did not have time to mourn the dreams she had given up or to wallow in self-pity. Her efforts to be a diligent homemaker were noticed by many of the young men in the area. To no one's surprise, she received many marriage proposals. She turned them all down, however, because she still felt that she had a religious calling. When she was twenty, she approached her mother about entering a convent. Although Isabelle was recovering from her illness, she was not ready to lose another family member and said no. However, Isabelle knew she could not deny God the life He had called into service. Five years later, her depression having subsided, Isabelle gave her daughter permission to enter the convent.

Although she once had intended to enter the Carmelite cloister, Guérin instead joined a relatively new order, the Sisters of Providence, becoming known as Sister Saint Theodore. The group that became the Sisters of Providence began as a group of lay women who did good works by teaching catechism and ministering to the needs of the sick during the war years. In this time people had grown indifferent to the practice of their faith, and through their example, the children followed suit. Father Jacques-François Dujarié realized that in the first years after the revolution it would be important to rebuild the faith of the land, especially in the French countryside. Father Dujarié planned to recruit a corps of women who would reside in a small two-room cottage. They named their venture La Petite Providence, or Little Providence, located in Ruillé-sur-Loir, about 225 miles southeast of Etables, and over the years the community grew as more women wanted to participate in the good works performed by the mission. They were given basic religious education, and in 1806 Father Dujarié

Sisters of Providence Motherhouse, Ruillé, France

decided that the time had come to convert the mission into a full-fledged religious community.

Father Dujarié composed the list of initial guidelines for the women to follow, including poverty, chastity, and obedience, but an additional vow encouraged the education of young girls and the care of the sick and poor. He named Mother Marie Madeleine (formerly Julie Josephine Zoë du Roscoät) to the post of superior general in 1818. After serving as the superior for four years Mother Marie Madeleine died of typhoid in June 1822. Sister Cecile (formerly Aimée Lecor) succeeded her, taking the name Mother Mary. For forty-three years she was the guiding force behind the order that shaped and molded many young sisters, including Guérin. To many, Mother Mary is considered to be the cofounder of the Sisters of Providence at Ruillé. Under her leadership the order was formally recognized and incorporated, which gave the sisters some legal existence.

Mother Mary appealed to Bishop Jean-Baptiste Bouvier of Le Mans for help in constructing a document that would outline the laws and procedures to stand as a directive for the community. The result was the Rule of 1835. Written by Bishop Bouvier, the Rule was one hundred pages of rules and regulations for the infant congregation. Similar to the mission statements of today, the Rule stated the purpose of the community: "to honor Divine Providence and to second its merciful designs on mankind by devoting themselves to the instruction of young girls and to the care of the unfortunate, whether in their homes, in prisons or in hospitals." In accordance with the fourth vow constructed by Father Dujarié, each establishment was to operate a free school, open after regular classes in order to teach domestic skills to poor children, along with a pharmacy on the premises from which the sisters would be able to dispense medical treatments. The Rule also put the sisters under the authority of the bishop of Le Mans, who took care of the community under his blanket of protection. The sisters were asked to renew their vows every five years, but the bishop waived that and, with permission, individual members could profess perpetual vows.

Mother Mary Lecor

Guérin possessed a maturity level that served her well. Mother Mary recognized the novice's talent and potential, and as she progressed, she was given more important jobs within the community. There was such a need for religious in the community that Mother Mary received many requests to open new houses and sent some of her novices to fill the void. One of Guérin's earliest assignments as a novice was teaching in the little town of Preuilly, at the Sisters of Providence establishment of Preuilly-sur-Claise.

After she professed her first vows in September 1825, Guérin was named the superior of an establishment in Saint Aubin at Rennes, 150 miles northwest of Ruillé in 1826. The students there were con-

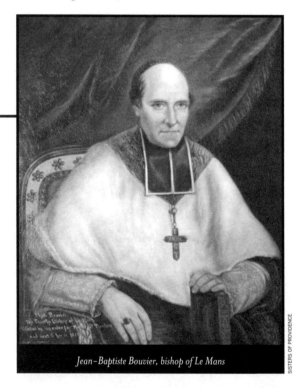

Jean-Baptiste Bouvier, bishop of Le Mans

sidered unruly and difficult. It was not the kind of institution that most would have enjoyed, but Guérin quickly accepted it, setting out to win the children over. She opened her arms to them, dealt with them fairly, and earned their respect. Once the students came around, their parents followed suit. She was loved by the establishment and enjoyed her work within it.

Guérin was so successful at Saint Aubin that it came as a shock to everyone when she was transferred to the small establishment of Soulaines in the Diocese of Angers. Although it was not uncommon for sisters to be transferred, Guérin's transfer was not without controversy. When the Sisters of Providence were founded in 1806, all of their assets were under the control of Father Dujarié, who managed not only his own funds but also the assets of a community of brothers. The sisters became concerned that their corporation could be responsible for any debts incurred by the brothers if both communities remained under the same umbrella. Although there was no sign that either the brothers or Father Dujarié would be anything other than frugal, Mother Mary appealed to the Most Reverend Philippe Carron, who was the bishop of Le Mans at the time, and asked him to separate the communities for business reasons. The bishop saw the sense in the proposal and approved the separation of finances, giving Mother Mary control of the economic resources of the Sisters of Providence.

With her sharp business sense, there is little doubt that Guérin saw the purpose in separating the two congregations. Nevertheless, she had a fondness for Father Dujarié and remained caring and sympathetic to him during his old age and illness, which some of the sisters considered disloyal to the order. The community's only recourse for this perceived disloyalty seemed to be to remove Guérin from the position that she loved. In time, the sisters fully exonerated her of any wrongdoing, but the misunderstanding remained a sore subject for many years. Guérin was deeply hurt, but was comforted by the support she received from the bishops and the sisters in the community, making her pain a little easier to bear.

Guérin was well liked at Soulaines, quickly gaining confidence and respect during her tenure. She persuaded a benefactor to contribute to the building of a new church in the community and was even accorded a medal for her educational excellence there. She spent most of her spare time studying scripture and spirituality, medicine, and pharmacology.

On the other side of the Atlantic Ocean, Bishop Simon Bruté was taming the wild land of Indiana. In 1834 he was named the bishop of the Vincennes diocese, which encompassed not only all of

Indiana, but the eastern third of Illinois as well. Simon Guillaume Gabriel Bruté de Rémur was born in Rennes, France, on March 20, 1779, into an affluent family. However, the death of Bruté's father when Bruté was only seven years old left the family's finances in turmoil. Bruté's mother sheltered priests in their apartment during the revolution, watching as the priests said daily Mass on a secret altar. Bruté even carried the Eucharist to imprisoned priests, traveling in the company of another priest who posed as a baker bringing food to a hungry prisoner.

Bruté eventually studied at the College of Medicine in Paris, where he was a very good student. A number of his professors achieved fame for their contributions to the study of chemistry, anatomy, and surgery, as well as to the humane treatment of the insane. Just before his graduation in 1802, Bruté was awarded the Corvisart Prize for outstanding work. Such a prize guaranteed him a successful career as a physician. However, Bruté refused the prize and announced that he planned to enter the priesthood. Although his mother was a devout Catholic, she opposed his decision to enter the seminary. Bruté tried to convince her that "if it was noble to become a doctor who cured illness of the body, it was even more nobler to cure the illnesses of the soul." Sadly, his mother was not convinced.

Bruté entered the Seminary of Saint Sulpice in Paris in 1804. At age twenty-five, he was older than most of the other seminarians. He was also different from others because of his background as a physician as well as the fact that the new emperor, Napoléon, seemed to have an interest in him, appointing him as the master of ceremonies for the Cardinal Archbishop of Paris. Though Bruté's mother was still against the idea of her son becoming a priest, she hoped that his vocation would lead him into an area where his background in medicine would be of some use. Bruté, on the other hand, was contemplating a career as a foreign missionary.

After his ordination in June 1808, he met with Father Benedict Joseph Flaget, a former missionary at Fort Vincennes, the French settlement on the Wabash River. A military post was constructed in the early eighteenth century, and by the middle of the century the Jesuits had built a church there. Very few priests had ministered to the people of Indiana and Illinois. Impressed with the stories he heard from Father Flaget, Father Bruté decided to go to the American missions and see how he could best minister to the people. He left for America with Bishop Flaget on June 10, 1810.

Sadly, Father Bruté's zeal to become a missionary and his superiors' vision were two different things. While he longed to work with the poorest of the poor, he was often assigned to teach. His first position was at Mount Saint Mary's in Emmitsburg, Maryland. Father Bruté found it difficult to teach without the massive library he had acquired while a seminarian in France, and he struggled to learn English. Writing to Flaget, who had become a bishop, Bruté said, "I am trying to learn practically my English. I have said Mass and preached, bad preaching as it may be, in six different places. This must force this dreadful English into my backward head, or I must renounce forever to know it." While he did learn to write in English, Father Bruté never became proficient in the language.

Privately, Father Bruté was not sure he wanted to stay in America. He wrote to his superiors asking for a transfer, but for years he struggled with the pull to a missionary's life. As his reputation as a pastor and a theologian grew, he became the spiritual adviser for Elizabeth Ann Seton (who would later be canonized) in October 1833. The bishops at the Second Provincial Council of Baltimore also sent his name to Rome in order for him to become bishop of a new diocese to be erected in Indiana and eastern Illinois, the Diocese of Vincennes. Father Bruté did not want to become a bishop and did not feel he could do the job. At the age of fifty-four, he felt he was already too old and made several excuses as to why he should not be appointed to the position, the heart of which was that he did not feel he had any administrative ability. Despite his arguments, he was named the first bishop of the new diocese in July 1834.

Bishop Bruté looked for members of the religious community to help him from the moment he arrived in the Diocese of Vincennes after his consecration in Saint Louis on October 28, 1834. Homesteaders, many of them Catholics from Germany, France, and Ireland, were flocking to the Midwest. Many were indifferent to their faith or neglected their religious practices because missionaries could only visit them sporadically. Bishop Bruté hoped to provide the diocese with more churches and schools.

Bishop Bruté finally had the missionary career he had dreamed of in France. He realized that he needed to find additional priests and funds to work throughout the large diocese. Determined to populate the area with proper Catholic communities, he sailed to France in 1835 to appeal for priests and clergy to anchor the diocese. Twenty priests responded to his call, and most of them were from Brittany. One of his priests was Father Edward Sorin, who founded the University of Notre Dame. Bishop Bruté also asked for an assistant to help oversee the diocese and to serve as his replacement if needed. His second-in-command as vicar general was Father Celestine de la Hailandière, a former judge who had become a priest in 1825. Bishop Bruté returned to Vincennes in 1836.

With several priests in place, Bishop Bruté knew he needed a community of sisters willing to travel to Indiana and help set up and run establishments founded in the diocese. By the time he had visited the land that became known as Saint Mary-of-the-Woods in 1837, he believed that some day a religious community would take root there. However, Bishop Bruté had a difficult time finding just the right group of women to come to the diocese. Suffering

Simon Bruté, first bishop of Vincennes

25

from tuberculosis made more severe by riding on horseback to visit all areas of the diocese, he knew time was running short, and he asked Father Hailandière to go to France in his place. While Father Hailandière was gone, Bishop Bruté died. Hailandière was appointed bishop of the Vincennes diocese, a position he neither expected nor wanted.

Eager to find just the right group of women for the trip to Indiana, Bishop Hailandière called at the motherhouse of Ruillé looking for volunteers for the mission. Although his request was unusual, Mother Mary did not refuse. In fact, she already seemed to know who might be the perfect person to travel to America. "We have only one Sister capable of making the foundation," she told Hailandière. "If she consents, we shall send you Sisters next summer." She was referring to Guérin.

Although Mother Mary already knew the woman she had in mind for the mission to America, she decided to ask for volunteers for the task. Surprisingly, Guérin, now in her forties, did not volunteer. She thought the project was worthwhile, but felt that she was too old and her health too poor to be of any good in America. Mother Mary took her aside and expressed that without Guérin at the helm, the entire mission might be scrubbed. Guérin agreed to go.

Travel plans were under way at once, preparing Guérin and her companions—Sister Saint Vincent Ferrer Gagé, Sister Basilide Sénéschal, Sister Olympiade Boyer, Sister Mary Xavier Lerée, and Sister Mary Liguori Tiercin—for their ocean voyage. In the spring of 1840, Bishop Hailandière wrote to Mother Mary and informed her that the diocese would pay for the sisters' passage, but beyond that, they would have to rely on Providence for their needs. He mentioned in his letter that there were plans to build a home for them, but the small frame church in the village had been destroyed in a fire, leaving little to greet them when they arrived.

Many decisions had to be made before the sailing. Mother Mary, Bishop Bouvier, and Bishop Hailandière had to determine how the sisters would be separated from their motherhouse in Ruillé. Bishop Hailandière told Bishop Bouvier that he had no problem taking on the responsibility of the sisters. "If you wish, Monsignor . . . I have no serious objection to make. I expressed a contrary wish in the fear that the sisters might be discouraged by the thought of no longer belonging to Ruillé," he wrote to Bishop Bouvier. Mother Mary also told Guérin about the role she was to play in Indiana: superior of the motherhouse in Indiana and the superior general to all of the surrounding establishments.

Meanwhile, Guérin attended the sisters' annual retreat. Mother Mary wrote her that she would be leaving for America on July 15, 1840. Mother Mary confided her feelings about the upcoming journey: "My hand trembles, my dear Theodore, my heart beats and my tears flow as I write you these words which may be the last I shall say to you. . . . I have always loved you from the bottom of my heart, and I always will love you." She went on to tell Guérin that Bishop Hailandière was advancing the funds to transport the sisters to New York, where a priest would meet them and provide them with the necessary means to complete the journey. All Guérin had to do now was count the days and wait.

Chapter 3

The Journey to the New World

On July 12, 1840, Sister Theodore Guérin and two of her traveling companions stepped into the carriage that would transport them to the seaside town of Le Havre. In Le Havre the group would board the *Cincinnati*, its transportation across the Atlantic Ocean to the sisters' new home in America. In the rush to depart at nine o'clock in the evening, the sisters only had time for one last blessing in the chapel and one last embrace with those who meant the most to them. Guérin compared leaving her homeland to the moment "of death." Her thoughts as she departed were of her younger sibling, Marie-Jeanne, who she was not able to see before she left. Unlike the others in the group, Guérin did not

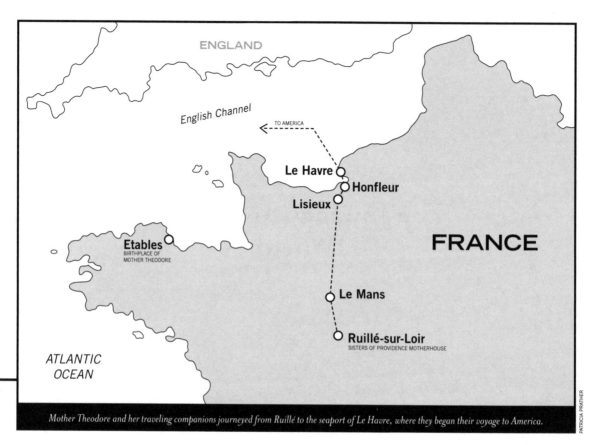

ENGLAND

English Channel

TO AMERICA →

Le Havre ○
○ Honfleur
Lisieux ·

Etables ○
BIRTHPLACE OF
MOTHER THEODORE

FRANCE

○ Le Mans

○ Ruillé-sur-Loir
SISTERS OF PROVIDENCE MOTHERHOUSE

ATLANTIC
OCEAN

Mother Theodore and her traveling companions journeyed from Ruillé to the seaport of Le Havre, where they began their voyage to America.

PATRICIA PRATHER

leave her parents behind, as her mother, Isabelle, had died in May 1839.

The weather was gloomy as the group left the motherhouse. Guérin later wrote that it was as if all of France was mourning the loss of its daughters. As they traveled, the beautiful French countryside spread out before them, and they were reminded again of all that they were leaving behind. More than one of them probably wondered if the mission was worth it.

The sisters completed the fifty-mile trip to Le Mans the following morning where they were joined by Sister Saint Vincent Ferrer Gagé and Sister Basilide Sénéschal. That afternoon, they celebrated Mass before they left for Le Havre, stopping in Lisieux,

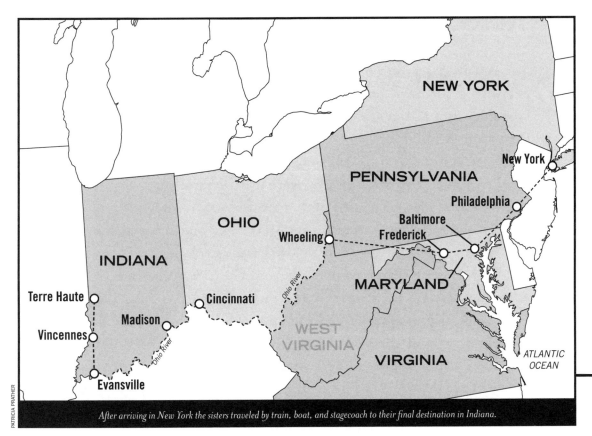

After arriving in New York the sisters traveled by train, boat, and stagecoach to their final destination in Indiana.

the hometown of Saint Therese of the Little Flower about fifty miles away. To pass the time in the coach, Guérin read through her correspondence. The sisters spent the night there before leaving for Honfluer, at the mouth of the Siene, the next morning. From Honfluer, Guérin could see the ocean, and when she looked at it, possibly feeling some trepidation about the upcoming voyage, she had a panic attack. She later wrote, "I nearly fainted. My eyes were covered with a mist, and there was a ringing in my head. I do not know what caused me to experience this painful sensation." However, she soon recovered.

This nausea was only the start of the violent bouts of motion sickness she experienced on the open sea. As the *Cincinnati* slipped from its harbor and moved toward the ocean on July 27, she was overcome by a wave of nervousness and sadness. "It would be difficult to describe what passed in my soul when I felt the vessel beginning to move and I realized I was no longer in France," Guérin wrote in her journal. "It seemed as if my soul were being torn from my body."

She was not the only one feeling homesick. There were fifty-eight passengers on the ship who were leaving family and friends in order to start a new life. Two of them were Jewish, one of whom was a rabbi. There were German immigrants and the Brassier family, with whom Guérin developed a close bond. Each of these travelers had broken ties to their homelands, and Guérin could understand their loss because she still felt her own so sharply.

Sadness soon was replaced by the powerful feeling of seasickness that plagued the sisters and passengers throughout the trip. Guérin chronicled how she and the sisters were unable to eat or to do much of anything except lie in bed. Their nausea was so bad that they could not even use the berths that were provided for them to sleep in. Rather, they put their mattresses on the floor and slept there. As one sister improved, she ministered to the others before the next wave of ill health hit her. "You never saw such a comedy," Guérin wrote. For two days, only Sister Basilide tended the others while she battled with her own bouts of nausea. The ship's captain did not speak French, so the sisters had to resort to hand gestures in order to get any assistance that they needed. The lack of communication did not seem to bother the sisters, who were too ill to converse anyway.

During one of her reprieves from illness, Guérin went up to the deck of the ship to admire the natural cathedral that was before her. Once the ship sailed beyond the Irish coastline, she watched the other ships passing and was amazed at how the vessels brought life to the sea. Her trips above the decks were reminiscent of her fascination with the sea as a child, when she would go to the seashore and dream of the day she would one day travel on the vast ocean. One day she counted twenty-five or thirty ships on the Atlantic, but there were no French vessels among them.

If Guérin found life beyond the ship interesting, it was nothing compared to life on board. Just after dinner one day, the captain was summoned to the cargo hold of the ship. "We did not know the cause of his sudden departure," she wrote, "but all at once we saw coming up from the hold three men with pallid and wicked countenances, trembling as though they were at the foot of the scaffold. These half-naked men were robbers who had escaped from prison and hidden themselves in our vessel, evading the researches of the police." The captain threatened to toss the men overboard, but he was a compassionate man and instead brought them to the decks and put them to work on the ropes. Guérin was put off by the men's appearance, and she never quite got over her uneasy feeling about them. She watched as they ate their biscuits while they worked and noted the captain's kindness to them. He ultimately paid for their passage on an English ship that was heading for Le Havre. Guérin was hardly sorry to see them go. "His hair was a half a foot in length," she wrote about one stowaway. "His face so dirty and repulsive, and at the same time so villainous, one could not but have a feeling of fear on beholding him."

Guérin learned that life on the sea was no pleasure cruise. For several days the ocean experienced a great calm in which the various ships appeared motionless on the water. The sea could be very fickle, however, and on August 5 a northeast wind blew in and stirred up an already troubled sea. As the winds increased, the waves grew and created a racket inside the ship that worried the sisters a great deal. "The poor ships, awhile ago so tranquil, were driven about and seemed on the verge of sinking," she wrote. "The waves appeared like mountains that came to bury us in the depths." As the hurricane crashed about them and threatened their voyage, Guérin prayed that she and the sisters' lives would be spared. The storm was so bad that the sisters could neither stand nor kneel. Guérin became sick again with a fever that she worried might kill her before she ever reached America. "It was extremely painful to be sick on an American ship which was lacking everything, even good water," she wrote.

During a reprieve from the storms, Guérin spotted a ship in the distance with a French flag unfurled. The sight of a ship from her homeland cheered her greatly, but for the most part, the days that passed on the ocean were identical. "We said our prayers in common and made our spiritual reading. Whenever I was able to be up we all passed our days on deck," she reported. Still, little incidences onboard kept life from becoming too mundane. "It takes so little on shipboard to produce a sensation," Guérin wrote in her journal. On one occasion a fire broke out, caused by the carelessness of a sailor who spilled the contents of his pipe. Luckily, the fire was contained. A more gruesome episode involved Guérin arriving on deck to discover that the billows were spattered in blood. The sea had claimed yet another victim. "Do not be alarmed," she wrote, using the humor she would become so well known for. "It was only a fish which had been caught with the harpoon, a sea hog (porpoise) so large that six of our vigorous sailors were hardly able to drag it aboard. . . . It struggled so violently that no one dared approach it; but at last one soldier braver than the rest, evidently a butcher by trade, ventured, and cut its throat with a knife, thus finishing the work."

The hardest part about life on the ship was being without the sacraments and not being able to attend Mass on a regular basis. Guérin and the sisters read the Ordinary of Mass together each Sunday, but it was not the same. There were moments in which she feared that they would die before ever receiving the sacraments again. "Instead of ringing of the merry bells, we had the rumbling of the waves; for the chants of the Church, we heard only the rough voices of the sailors," she wrote.

Guérin wrote in her journal about some of the passengers on the ship. She developed a close relationship with Thomas Brassier, his wife, and their six children. Guérin was so impressed by the family that she asked Thomas to come and work for her in the Vincennes diocese. He agreed, and it was decided that he would wait in New York until Guérin forwarded him the money to travel to Indiana. He would pay her investment back out of his wages. Guérin also got along well with the German rabbi, although they did not speak the same language. Guérin was pleased that he did not look upon her with disdain, but was rather kind, once bringing her an orange when she was bedridden with seasickness.

Later in the journey, the winds picked up and the sails unfurled, carrying the ship across the water at roughly about eight knots per hour. Guérin and her companions tried to keep their balance, but she said that the vessel "rolled about like a nut on the sea." The motion was so terrible that they could not even keep a candle burning without it tipping over and threatening to burn the lot of them. "When it leaned to the right, it drew our beds and all that was in the room to that side; then, regaining its equilibrium, it threw us with equal violence to the left," she wrote. The sisters struggled to move about the ship to no avail, crashing into one another with unexpected force. There was simply no way to navigate the unsteady boat. Thankfully, the sisters were blessed with a sense of humor that helped them laugh in difficult moments, as when the sisters had to crawl up to breakfast on their hands and knees. Guérin said that "when a vessel is thus tossed about, it is surprising to feel one's self lifted up by the air, and then to feel an enormous weight which seems to crush one down like grapes in the wine press."

Just as the sisters arrived at the banks of Newfoundland on August 22, another storm hit. The sisters were sick once again, especially

Sister Saint Vincent Ferrer, who had suffered throughout the voyage. According to Guérin's journal, the sisters were not the only ones afraid during this time. The other passengers also feared for their safety as they watched the captain and officers work nonstop to keep the ship secure. Even the rabbi had his faith shaken in the storm.

Not long after this storm, the ship entered the bay that took them to New York. The following morning, the sisters saw land and rejoiced that their journey at sea was nearly completed. On September 4, perhaps expecting a vast wilderness, Guérin was surprised to see that America had homes, settlements, and beautifully landscaped properties that seemed to reach out to the sisters and welcome them "home." "'At last we have arrived,' we said to one another," when they arrived in New York. "'The perils of the sea are passed!' We threw ourselves on our knees, and with hearts full of gratitude we offered our thanks to God for all the benefits He had bestowed on us," Guérin chronicled.

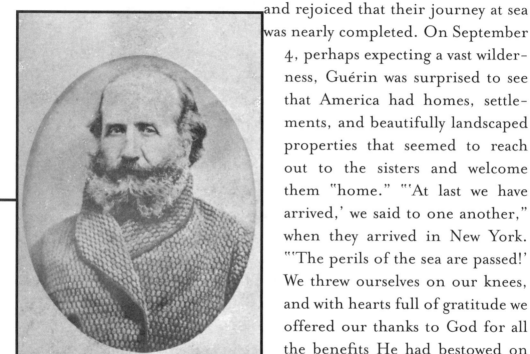

Samuel Byerley

While they were quarantined for several days on the ship, Guérin watched the Americans waiting on the dock for their loved ones to disembark. She knew that the passengers would be happy to see their loved ones again, but she knew that she and her sisters might not fare so well. She was aware that many Americans would be unhappy with her arrival and would treat her with indifference and contempt. It was a cross she had to bear, and she was determined to make the best of whatever situation God handed her.

When they finally were allowed to disembark, Guérin did not know where to go or what to do. She had no experience with obtaining lodging and was a little leery about staying in New York. There was also the language barrier. She was not even sure how to arrange for their luggage to be taken from the ship. She assumed there would be some representative from the Vincennes diocese waiting for her, but none arrived. However, the sisters did have assistance in the New York harbor. Doctor Sidney Doane, the quarantine officer, spoke French and assisted them at the quarantine station, gave them fruit, and delivered their letter to the bishop. Samuel Byerley, a New York merchant, assisted with the sisters' baggage when they landed in New York and again with the packing and shipping of their baggage from New York to Saint Mary-of-the-Woods.

Sylvia Parmentier

37

Realizing the sisters' dilemma, the bishop of New York sent Father Felix Varela, the vicar general of New York, to escort the sisters to the home of Sylvia Parmentier, who lived in Brooklyn and often took in missionaries passing through New York on their way to establishments elsewhere. The sisters quickly won over their new acquaintances during their five-day stay. Parmentier and Byerley arranged for the luggage to be delivered from the ship without subjecting it to the inspection at the customhouse.

Guérin also felt that she owed a great deal of gratitude to Father Varela, who was sent as sort of a companion for the sisters. She wrote of his kindness to the congregation not only when they landed in New York but also during their stay in Brooklyn, helping the sisters get used to their new country. "This reverend gentleman did not stop there, but carried his charitable attentions so far as to send a devout young Englishman to accompany us to Philadelphia," she wrote. Because the man could not speak French, Father Varela also provided a translator to help the sisters communicate.

While Guérin had a great deal of affection for the people she encountered during her journey, she also had many opinions of her new homeland. She thought New York possessed a depressive attractiveness that did not appeal to her. She was unaccustomed to the grouping of similar businesses in various districts and to the wide streets, which people only crossed at corners. She also could not get over the fact that Americans were so extravagant in their religious life. Guérin felt the faithful were pious, but they did not dress appropriately for Mass. She also did not like the amount of music that was played in the service. "The Mass and Vespers were sung to music, which . . . did not particularly please me," Guérin wrote. "I had a great deal more devotion in our poor barn at Soulaines, notwithstanding the lack of harmony there."

She also felt that the churches in America were too small and poorly built. She was disappointed in the large numbers of Protestant churches in the area as opposed to the Catholic ones, and as she looked at their towering steeples, she began to realize how difficult her mission would be. "There are churches for at least fourteen or fifteen different sects, but not one is sheltered by the saving sign of the cross," she said.

After all of their belongings were secured and on their way to the final destination, the sisters traveled by train to Philadelphia, where they arrived in the afternoon and were immediately taken to Bishop Francis Patrick Kenrick. He greeted them warmly and offered them lodging with the Sisters of Charity. Although the two communities did not speak the same language, they found ways to communicate. Guérin was impressed with her hostesses, calling them "model religious," and said she could only hope to live up to their example.

The sisters hoped that there would be a letter from Bishop Celestine de la Hailandière waiting in Philadelphia, but Bishop Kenrick told them that no such letter had arrived. Guérin recalled, "This Reverend gentleman informed us that the Bishop of Vincennes had not sent anyone to meet us, and that he himself had written that it was unnecessary. The brave Father told us that we could travel very well without knowing English, that it was not indispensable. However, after reflecting on the matter, I decided not to set out alone, and the Bishop of Philadelphia approved my decision; consequently, Father Freynaye [M. A. Frenaye was not a priest but rather Bishop Kenrick's agent] and I wrote to Bishop de la Hailandière that we would remain there until someone came for us."

With nothing to do but wait for a reply from Bishop Hailandière, the sisters took in the sights of the city. Guérin found Philadelphia more to her liking than New York. "We went out twice to view the surrounding country . . . there are superb hills, on whose sloping sides are beautiful English gardens, and here and there houses of a pleasing style," she wrote. "But what adds most to the beauty of this part of the country is the magnificent river at the foot of the hills, gliding along so tranquilly that one would take it for a small lake rather than a river." Perhaps she also enjoyed the little bit of fame she experienced in the City of Brotherly Love. The French settlers in the area visited the sisters often and made quite a fuss over the community. Bishop Kenrick was also a frequent caller.

As they continued to wait on a letter from Bishop Hailandière, the president of the Terre Haute Bank offered to escort the sisters to their next stop in Baltimore. The sisters were considering his offer when they met a French priest by the name of William Chartier, who was traveling from Canada to Vincennes. They decided to travel with him and left for Baltimore on Friday, September 18. Just before their departure, Guérin received word that some money had been forwarded to Thomas Brassier, per her agreement with him on the ship. He would use the money to go to the Vincennes diocese and work off the debt in whatever way the sisters needed him to. As she traveled by train to Baltimore, Guérin was once again amazed with rail travel in America. She commented in her journal that it was impossible to describe the country that they had just traveled because it had passed by so quickly despite the fact that it would still be a month before they would arrive in Terre Haute.

In Baltimore, one hundred and sixty miles away from Philadelphia, the sisters once again enjoyed the hospitality and kindness of the Sisters of Charity. The language barrier again limited them, but the two communities threw caution to the wind, testing their language skills with each other. Guérin quickly learned how easily mistakes could be made. "Not one of the Sisters knew French," she wrote. "The Superior seeing our weariness tried to ask in French if we wanted to go to bed. She said instead *etre cocher* (to be a coachman). I, on my part, called her a negro. I do not know what I was trying to say. See what it is to be in a country without knowing the language. It is surely disagreeable and exposes one to grave inconvenience."

During their brief stay in Baltimore, Guérin and the others had the opportunity once again to do some sightseeing. Guérin did not find the city to be as charming as Philadelphia. She called the cathedral "the finest monument of architecture consecrated to Catholic worship in the United States," but found other churches too oppressive. The city itself was not to her liking either. "The streets are extremely wide and the city is very extensive. The people make you take endless walks telling you all the while, 'It is quite near, just on the next street,'" she wrote.

The congregation next traveled by train to Frederick, Maryland, and arrived in the afternoon on Saturday. In Frederick the congregation was the guest of the former superior general of the Sisters of Charity, Mother Rose White. Mother Rose shared the stories of the beginnings of her institute and how it struggled in its earliest years. Over time, she said, the establishment developed into a community that educated the orphaned as well as teaching the more affluent children at their academy. No doubt her stories were of some comfort to Guérin, who wondered if her little group would succeed in its new venture.

After their overnight stay in Frederick, the sisters headed for the Ohio River through the Allegheny Mountains. During this leg of the journey the sisters were advised to change from their habits to secular clothing because they were entering country where they would be more susceptible to prejudice and bigotry. Guérin thought it was better to be safe rather than sorry. As they traveled, Guérin thought that they passed through some of the prettiest country she had seen yet with its wild beauty and high, green hills along rivers. "Every moment unveiled new beauties," Guérin wrote. "At every turn new grandeurs rose before us."

There was also a certain amount of danger as they moved forward. Traveling through the mountains was never safe, especially in a stagecoach. One wrong move by the team could send a group of passengers plummeting to their deaths. It was not only the precipices that concerned Guérin, but also the danger of bandits who hid in the mountains and pounced on the unsuspecting. Therefore the sisters traveled both day and night in order to protect themselves.

Upon arrival in Wheeling, Virginia (present-day West Virginia), the sisters took a small steamboat to travel for four days on the Ohio River en route to Cincinnati. On the steamboat Guérin experienced a surprise attack from an enemy she never expected to encounter. "We were far from supposing that, in the midst of the city where we had been so well received, we were to find a multitude of enemies athirst for the blood of the French. Until then we had not fought until the shedding of blood, but this was a night of slaughter," she wrote. "I may say without boasting too much that several of my enemies perished by my hands, but I was sorely wounded. All of my Sisters, except Sister Basilide, bore glorious scars which proved that they, too, had undergone a bloody battle with mosquitoes."

If Guérin had a sense of humor regarding the mosquitoes, she most certainly lost it after their arrival in Madison, Indiana, on September 22. Bishop Hailandière was making a pastoral visit at the time of their arrival, but when they disembarked, the sisters learned that the bishop had gone on to another mission. "We waited for him for two days in an inn where we nearly died of lonesomeness," she wrote.

The bishop finally arrived on October 1 and told the sisters that they would be settling a few miles from Terre Haute. Four postulants were waiting for them in addition to a chaplain, who was overseeing the construction of their new home. The bishop excused himself for not sending any of his priests to meet the sisters by saying they had all been too ill to travel. He personally escorted the sisters to the steamboat and told them that he would be joining them in two weeks. "It was a great comfort for us to have seen him even for so short a time, but we were quite sad to have to go to Vincennes without him. However, we had to make this sacrifice," Guérin wrote.

As they set out for their new settlement, their journey was delayed somewhat by storms that arrived in the area. Although they were used to the variety of dangers that always seemed to be around them, the sisters did not realize that they were only now facing the most treacherous miles of their journey. The sisters again traveled down the Ohio River, landing in Evansville, only fifty-five miles from Vincennes. Guérin was thrilled to be so close to their destination, but a conversation with a missionary priest may have given her second thoughts about the diocese as well as the establishment she was about to adopt as her own. The priest appeared to be in his late twenties and to be suffering from extreme poverty and destitution. Guérin was so shocked by his appearance that she told him his housekeeper was not taking care of him properly. When the young man informed her that he did not have a housekeeper, Guérin asked him who took care of the housework and other chores. He replied that he and his companion were given their daily ration from a local baker and that his accommodations were very primitive. For the first time Guérin had a sense of what might be in store for her upon her arrival to her new home.

The group traveled by stagecoach to Vincennes, quickly realizing that the area they were to inhabit was unlike the sections of country they had traveled through. The wide streets, homes, and other reminders of larger towns and cities were replaced by dense forests, rough roads, and the occasional farmhouse. At one point the stage stopped and the sisters spent the night with a farmer and his family. The following day they arrived in Vincennes and were taken to the Sisters of Charity, where they were able to dress in their habits and visit the local cathedral. "What a Cathedral!" Guérin wrote. "Our barn at Soulaines is better ornamented and more neatly kept." The poverty of the country was more than she could bear, and she cried openly. Her journals reveal that she did not see much of a future for Vincennes, a city in such an underdeveloped part of the country. She had to wonder what awaited her in Terre Haute.

The sisters planned to leave for Terre Haute on October 17,

but bad weather postponed their departure. Sister Basilide fell ill, and although Guérin suggested that they wait until her health improved, Sister Basilide insisted that they leave. They traveled in the dark on roads that were sometimes impassable due to washed-out bridges and potholes. "It was not without danger that we were traveling, especially in the night; in fact, we had gone only six miles when the stagecoach was upset in a deep mud hole, throwing us head foremost," Guérin wrote.

The stagecoach was stuck in the mud, and the sisters had a great deal of difficulty trying to get out of the carriage. When the stagecoach was pulled from the mud, the sisters continued on with their journey but spent the night in a farmhouse when it was clear the weather wasn't going to cooperate that evening.

The following morning, Guérin and her companions once again boarded the coach that would take them the short distance to the Wabash River where they could catch a ferry to the opposite bank. The forest was flooded and trees had fallen causing a great deal of difficulty for the horses to navigate, but the animals continued forward. Guérin wondered if they might yet perish when they were so close to their final destination. "I may say, however, that I was not at all alarmed," she wrote. "When one has nothing more to lose, the heart is inaccessible to fear. The water poured in on us. We thought we were surely gone this time; but the driver without losing his American coolness managed the horses so dexterously" that they were soon out of danger.

Once again rolling on solid ground, the sisters rode deep into the woods, and finally Father Stanislaus Buteux, who was to serve as the sisters' chaplain, announced that they had arrived. Guérin was astonished that she was surrounded by nothing but a forest with no village or home in sight. She discovered that there was only a primitive church with no tabernacle or missal stand, and virtually no altar making it a less-than-ideal-place for the sisters to stand before the Blessed Sacrament (a consecrated communion host constantly on display) and offer a prayer of thanksgiving for a safe arrival. She had to wonder about this land that she would one day call home.

Mother Mary Cecilia Bailly

Chapter 4

A New Home

When Sister Theodore Guérin saw the sisters' new home on October 22, 1840, Mother Mary Cecilia (formerly Eleanor Bailly), who followed Mother Theodore as the superior general of the congregation in 1856, later reported, "her strength failed her . . . it seemed to her that they came to bury themselves in the wilderness, for what prospect of a school where there were no families, no population?" Their primitive surroundings must have made her wonder how it would be possible to turn a forest location in the middle of nowhere into a functional institution for education. What would happen if she failed?

She was amazed at the sparseness of her new surroundings. Not only was there barely a church, but it was also furnished poorly. There were three planks draped with cloth to create a place where Mass was said as well as a small altar stone and a dark blue calico cloth protecting the pyx (a communion holder), chalice, and other Mass necessities. She was also surprised to learn that this rough structure measuring about thirteen feet wide by fifteen feet long served as a church, a chapel for the sisters, as well as the primary residence for the priest.

"The furniture consists of . . . a bed covered in mere rags, two little tables, one laden with books at the foot of the bed, the other in a corner serving as a writing-desk; there are besides, two old trunks, an old chair, and a small bench," Guérin wrote upon seeing her sparse surroundings.

She discovered that Father Stanislaus Buteux had an area of about sixty miles to attend to and that when he was not ministering to the needs of the community, he toiled on the production of the sisters' home just like any other worker.

Her spirit was renewed, however, after kneeling by the altar and submitting herself to the will of God. She met the four postulants who were waiting for her: Mary Doyle, Frances Theriac, Agnes Dukent, and Josephine Pardeillan. Two of these women were formerly members of the Sisters of Charity, but they were eager to begin their instruction as members of the Sisters of Providence and to work within the community.

The postulants had been living with a local farmer, Joseph Thralls, and his family. The family welcomed the new arrivals and showed them to a small room that had been given up for their use. They were also given half of a loft that was used to store corn. The room served as a bakery, refectory, recreation room, and infirmary, and the attic provided a place for the sisters to sleep. "It is so crowded that we have to dress ourselves on the beds [straw mattresses] and make them up one after the other," Guérin wrote. Their quarters not only were cramped, but also were subjected to the weather, as the shingles just above their attic room often let in the wind and the rain. Still, the sisters were grateful for a safe and relatively warm place to live while their home was under construction.

Within the first few days, the sisters began to learn about their new home. The settlement consisted only of a few log cabins in a dense forest. Each morning, the sisters walked to the little log chapel to pray before the Blessed Sacrament (a consecrated communion host constantly on display). They often walked through the woods in order to check on the progress of the building that was under construction to be used as a home for the sisters. The day after the sisters arrived, Guérin wrote about seeing her future convent, "Like the castles of the knights of old, it is so deeply hidden in the woods that you cannot see it until you come up to it," Guérin described. "It is a pretty two-story brick house, fifty feet wide by twenty-six feet deep. There are five large openings in front. The first stone was laid August seventeenth and it is already roofed . . . there are yet neither doors nor windows; all is being done, little by little."

During those first few days, the sisters discovered that the woods were full of berries, nuts, and medicinal plants that would be useful for a host of maladies. Guérin was also on the lookout for ways in which she could employ Thomas Brassier and his family. She wanted to honor her promise to him, and she finally decided that the Brassiers could clear part of the land so that the sisters could plant a vegetable garden.

Guérin was worried that she would not be able to do any good in Indiana, and she wrote Bishop Celestine de la Hailandière of her concerns. "It is astonishing that this remote solitude has been chosen for a novitiate and especially for an academy," Guérin wrote in her journal. "All appearances are against it. I have given

Diorama of the sisters' arrival at the log chapel at Saint Mary-of-the-Woods, 1840

my opinion frankly to the Bishop . . . and to all who have any interest in the success of our work. All have given reasons that are not entirely satisfactory; yet I dare not disregard them."

She had good reason to be worried. There was so much to do and so little to work with. The group also had to adjust to a very different lifestyle. She and the other sisters immediately began to learn English, while the postulants began their religious instruction. There were misunderstandings. Guérin wrote of one incident in her journal. "We had employed a young woman, an orphan, wretchedly poor and miserably clad to help us wash. . . . When dinner time came, there was my washerwoman sitting down at table with us. I was so indiscreet as to say it would be better for her not to take dinner with the Community," Guérin wrote. "I wish you could have seen the change in the countenances of our American postulants! I had to compromise by telling the girl she might eat with the reader at the second table. The mere name of 'servant' makes them revolt, and they throw down whatever they have in their hands and start off at once."

As winter approached, it was apparent that the convent would not be ready. Facing the harsh winter months with no finished home, a borrowed space, no opportunity for income, and a lack of food staples, Guérin feared this first winter could be the sisters' last. She wondered if the Thrallses would be willing to sell their farmhouse. The sisters could use the house as a convent, while the building under construction would be used for a school and provide income for the congregation. She presented the plan to Bishop Hailandière, and he saw the sense in the proposal. The bishop negotiated the deal, and Thralls agreed to sell his home, the surrounding land, and his farm animals for eighteen hundred dollars and moved to another location about a couple of miles away but still within the Saint Mary-of-the-Woods village. Members of the Thralls family still reside in that part of the state to this day.

Once the sisters were able to take over the entire house, the rooms still served multiple purposes. The sisters still used one of the rooms as an assembly, study, refectory, and infirmary, but the newly unoccupied spaces gave them space for a chapel in the large room. By November 27, 1840, the sisters were installed in their new home.

For the first time Guérin could see a purpose in her mission in Indiana. She wrote to Mother Mary Lecor, her superior in France, telling her of their good fortune and admitting that although the move may have been a hasty decision, it was the only reasonable solution that presented itself before a terrible winter arrived. She told Mother Mary about their new surroundings and described the culture that they had entered, not to mention the various plans for future establishments and some of her concerns. "The people are glad to see us and promise us pupils to learn French. You have no idea of all they teach here. Monseigneur [the bishop] said to me yesterday that it was specially to establish here the French religious spirit that he had asked for us," she wrote. "The most pressing concern for us was a lodging for the winter, we have bought the house where we are, which is, as I have already told you, a little farm house . . . otherwise we would have had neither house, nor field, nor orchard. . . . It was absolutely impossible to spend the winter, which is already very cold . . . in a cabin open to all the winds. . . . Now at least, however badly situated, we are 'chez nous.'"

In her letter, Guérin also mentioned that the bishop was planning for the sisters to address her as *Mère*, the French word for mother. The request gave Guérin a heavy heart because she still felt so attached to the community of Ruillé and her own mother superior who resided there. "This name gave me pain; then I found that it was to cost my Sisters, poor children, very much," she wrote. "What a mother they have! What a difference! Finally I forbade them to call me by that name. Mother would pain them less." When she responded, Mother Mary admonished the sister for sending her a letter about their voyage that seemed romantic in tone. She told Guérin that she would have preferred to read an account more pious in nature. It is clear from her words that she was less than enthusiastic about "Mother" Theodore's new title. "Although you bear the name of Mother, my dear Theodore, do not forget that you still belong to the Providence of Ruillé," Mother Mary's letter read.

December was a harsh month for the sisters. Although the community now numbered twelve, as two more postulants had joined them, Guérin fell critically ill on Christmas night. She was afflicted with violent headaches, fever, and fainting spells. Because her health was already frail, there was fear that she would not survive. The other sisters worried that if she died, their mission would fail. Other than at mealtimes, Bishop Hailandière stayed by her side, hearing her confession and anointing her. Each day she grew alarmingly worse and was bled often by a physician. Sister Saint Vincent Ferrer Gagé wrote about Guérin's trials, saying, "She was so ill . . . that the doctor having spent eight days near her gave her up, convinced that she would not live through the night. . . . During her illness the Sisters suffered intense anxiety for they saw no alternative if she died. The mission could not be continued, as she was the only one qualified by virtue and capacity to carry on the work and succeed in establishing a community under the existing circumstances." The bishop consistently prayed by Guérin's side, especially when all hope seemed to be lost. He was said to be immovable while he prayed fervently in the chapel.

Although it would be months before she fully recovered, Guérin began regaining her strength in January. By mid-February, she began thinking about the work that needed to be done for the coming spring. A successful crop would be vital for the sisters' survival the next winter and by the end of April in addition to potatoes, part of the land had been cleared to provide a place for radishes, lettuce, and onions. Thomas Brassier planted a variety of vegetables under the direction of Sister Basilide Sénéschal, and before long, the grounds were alive with chickens and at least one pig, not to mention a small orchard. Not wishing to remain a financial burden to the bishop, the congregation worked the land in order to become more self-sufficient. However, the bishop continued to harp about the sisters' expenditures, calling their needed items an "abyss" of expense.

It is unclear precisely when the difficulties between the bishop and Guérin began, but on May 1, 1841, she wrote to Augustine

Martin, the vicar general of the Diocese of Vincennes, asking for advice on how to deal with Bishop Hailandière. "I have followed exactly your recommendations in regard to the Bishop, and I have found them good," she wrote. He is an excellent father. I have never found a more compassionate heart, one more charitable, under so cold an exterior. One thing that deeply grieves my heart is the pain we give to him. So far there is nothing but complaints about us. I confide this to your paternity. . . . With a little patience, I hope all will go on well; but, in the meantime, we are under humiliation. Oh, good way for the proud, accustomed to be praised, admired, and carried along, and who now find themselves, like rejected stones, good for nothing!"

While there were some delays in the academy's opening, due primarily to funding, the sisters were more determined than ever to see an operational boarding school at Saint Mary's. Bishop Hailandière arrived in May 1841 to arrange for the workmen and to continue construction of the academy's building. In the days and weeks after he left, work progressed rapidly on the school, and the sisters were pleased that a target opening date of July was set.

By this time, there were sixteen members of the community with eight postulants and four novices. Sister Saint Vincent Ferrer was the mistress of novices but Guérin was still responsible for the education of the community. In a letter written to Mother Mary not long after Guérin recovered from her illness, she spoke of how inadequate she felt in trying to mentor an entire community. "To be a religious in France and to be one here are two things totally different, here where one must be able to say to one's dear companions at every instant 'Be what I am.' How terrifying that is, especially for me who am the furthest from this ideal."

For many of the missionary priests in the area, the arrival of the Sisters of Providence was welcome news. In the Midwest in 1841, educational facilities typically consisted of one-room schoolhouses.

Many children did not attend school on a regular basis, and early on, Guérin wrote to her superior in Ruillé about how the people were anxious to have the sisters in the diocese and promised them students. Before the sisters arrived in 1840, only about 50,000 children attended school. Almost immediately, priests asked the sisters to establish schools in their communities, but Guérin prudently thought it was wiser to get their own mission on sound footing before creating future establishments. She did, however, make a promise to send some sisters to Jasper as soon as she was able since Jasper was one of the original locations that Simon Bruté, the late bishop of Vincennes, longed to have sisters develop and maintain.

Jasper also offered one of the more well-developed communities in the area as well, so it was a natural selection for an early Sisters of Providence settlement. The priest in Jasper, Father Joseph Kundek, had already managed to build a solid church, a building to be used as a school, and had immediate accommodations available should the sisters decide to set up an establishment there.

As word spread that the sisters were opening a new school, Catholics and Protestants alike inquired about the school that Guérin modeled after the

Father Joseph Kundek

SISTER MARY BORROMEO BROWN, *THE HISTORY OF THE SISTERS OF PROVIDENCE*, VOL. 1 (NEW YORK: BENZIGER BROTHERS, 1949)

academies in France. According to all accounts, Guérin possessed all of the talents necessary to open and operate a French-based educational system. She encouraged her sisters to develop a relationship with their students in order to affect not only their minds but also their hearts. She stressed the importance of moving beyond basic textbooks and felt it appropriate to offer classes in practical skills that would help the students earn their way later in life. Most settlers were not used to a school that offered such an extensive curriculum. An advertisement in the *Terre Haute Wabash Courier* listed the courses and instruction that would be given. In addition to classes in reading, writing, and arithmetic, the Saint Mary-of-the-Woods Academy offered courses in geography, history, chemistry, botany, and mythology as well as instruction in a host of practical applications such as beading, lacework, and tapestry. Tuition for the academy was one hundred dollars per year with extra fees for music and art classes as well as nominal charges for mending and medicine. By June, three students were promised to the academy. Their names were Mary Lenoble, Sarah Williams, and Susan Lalumiere. Four more students joined them shortly thereafter.

One of the first students, Jane Brown, felt a special connection with Guérin. She wrote of the bond the two shared in one of her journals, saying that Guérin took her under her wing when she learned of Brown's desire to become a nun. Guérin guided Brown on her spiritual journey. Brown did become a nun, taking the name Sister Anastasie and was one of the order's superior generals. She later wrote that when she was a student at the academy, most of the teaching was conducted by Sister Basilide except for English, which was taught by Sister Ann Joseph who was an English-speaking novice. She noted that Guérin did teach classes from time to time and always took an interest in what was going on around the school, particularly in the mathematics department.

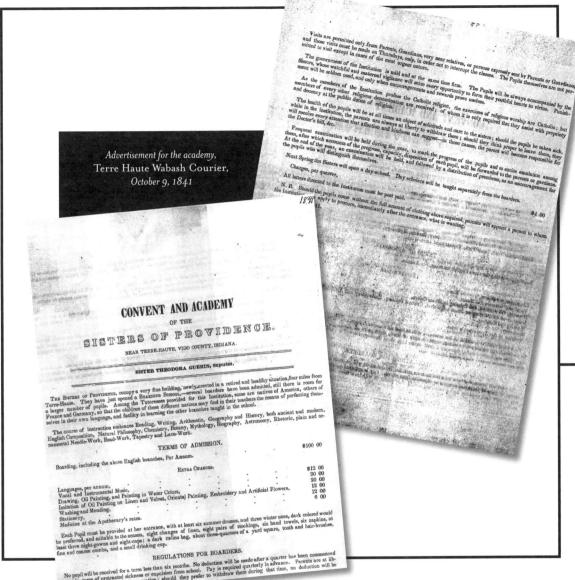

The bishop was very eager to see that the academy was successful. He bought books and nearly five hundred dollars worth of equipment to help the school get off the ground, including dishes, furniture, and lamps. He even went so far as to draw up a roster and list of individual duties for the sisters. Guérin was, of course, installed as the superior with Sister Aloysia Doyle serving as a substitute and Father Buteux offering music lessons. Sister Basilide, Sister Marie Joseph Pardeillan, and one of the American newcomers to the community were to focus on learning American customs in order to be able to move out to other establishments in the future. Other postulants and novices rounded out the rest of the faculty. Just after the summer retreat of 1841, Sister Saint Vincent Ferrer was named the superior of the academy but, not long after, the responsibility was too much for her since she was too timid for the job. Ultimately, Guérin took over the supervisory role.

The academy's early accommodations still left much to be desired. The bishop had ordered iron beds for the students, but the delivery of them was slow, and the sisters were not yet used to the hot Indiana summers. Despite the lack of comfort and convenience, they and the students plowed ahead with their duties, studying reading, spelling, math, and English along with classes in French and German. The children grew to love the sisters, especially Sister Basilide who gave drawing and painting lessons.

Because of the timing of the academy's opening, the first semester was destined to be a short one. As the sisters closed the doors at the end of the term in August and prepared for their annual retreat, they also began preparations for the next term, which would begin in a month. By the time the new term started, the issues that had delayed the opening of the academy were remedied. The beds had arrived and a prospectus had been published to let the settlers of the surrounding community know about the establishment and give them a sense of what the sisters had to offer their children. Students were expected to arrive with six summer dresses and three winter ones. Dark colors were requested. Each girl had to bring with her eight changes of linen, eight pairs of stockings, six hand towels, six napkins, three nightgowns and nightcaps at the minimum, a dark calico bag, personal items, yarn, and a small drinking cup. Visits were only allowed on Thursdays by parents, guardians, or those who were sent by parents. Students were not allowed to leave the campus at all. In the advertisement that ran in the *Wabash Courier* the charge for study at the academy per quarter was four dollars.

All things considered, as the sisters looked back on their inaugural year in Indiana, they had to be pleased with their efforts to establish a fine institution in a new land. Guérin and her companions had shown that they had the fortitude to survive a brutal voyage and the aptitude to adjust to frontier life. Despite all of their hard work and success at Saint Mary's, the congregation's first year in Indiana did not pass without controversy, conflict, or criticism. One key component was the sisters' chaplain, Father Buteux. He had a compulsion to meddle in the affairs of the sisters and was inclined to run the congregation according to his will rather than to guide the community as they needed him to do. He required the sisters to spend hours in his room for individual spiritual direction and concerned himself with the most trivial matters in the community. He went so far as to tell the sisters that they put too many vegetables in their soup, and the sisters were not allowed an extra handkerchief without his permission.

Bishop Hailandière did not know how far Father Buteux had gone with the congregation until various visitors to the community reported the priest's behavior toward the sisters. Father Buteux's issues with the community were potentially detrimental. Although he at first seemed only to be concerned for their work, that concern became a desire to maintain exclusive control over the sisters. Father Buteux was especially interested in the postulants who had preceded the sisters to Saint Mary's, and for some weeks before the sisters' arrival, the postulants had been under his direction alone. Father Buteux, feeling that Guérin was unsuited to serve as the foundress of a new congregation and believing that the mission would be better served by someone familiar with American customs, was grooming his own batch of hopefuls in order to take over the community and get rid of the French sisters once and for all.

Guérin did not know what to do, and realizing that Father Buteux agreed with her own concerns that she was not up to the task of leading the congregation only fueled her insecurity. At one point she discussed the possibility of resigning with Bishop Hailandière and Mother Mary. She wanted them to find someone more qualified for the job. She could not have realized she was playing right into Father Buteux's grand plan.

Bishop Hailandière was unaware of the situation until several members of the clergy reported that things had gotten out of control. Although the bishop removed Father Buteux from his post, the trouble did not end. Father Buteux continued to associate with the sisters and to write one, Sister Aloysia, the former Mary Doyle, without Guérin's knowledge. "The subject was the founding of a community according to his original plan, making his protégé the superior," Guérin later wrote. "The sister had herself spoken to four of the postulants and had them spoken to, to engage them to follow her in the spring." Guérin was so angry that she hitched up a buggy and set out for Vincennes in the dead of night in order to discuss the matter with the bishop face to face. The two of them concluded that it would be best for Sister Aloysia to leave the community rather than remain and cause a deeper rift.

The other issue that arose during this first year—who had the financial responsibility for the sisters—would plague the order for years to come. Guérin was in a constant state of confusion concerning under whose jurisdiction the community fell, and no one seemed to be able to give her a satisfactory answer. She knew that the bishop of Vincennes was doing all that he could for the sisters, but he was responsible for a vast diocese with commitments to many other sisters and priests, and he did not have the economic resources to finance Guérin's small community. She also knew that Mother Mary had her own financial obligations in Ruillé. Guérin did not want to have to go through the bishop for all of her needs, and she found that it was also very inconvenient to write to Europe each time a decision had to be made.

One misunderstanding arose when Mother Mary received an anonymous letter detailing life at Saint Mary-of-the-Woods. Not knowing that the letter was full of inaccuracies, Mother Mary confronted Guérin about the letter in December 1841. "A person entirely unknown to me but who seems to bear a sincere interest in our Congregation . . . writes to us from Cincinnati that the six Sisters we have sent to Vincennes are in the greatest difficulty and suffering. . . . What seems to me certain is, that this letter is from a friend with no pretensions other than for the glory of God." Mother Mary was concerned for those in Indiana and wanted to know what was happening in the fledgling establishment—Were they experiencing great difficulties? Were there problems? "What is to be done in the ignorance in which you leave us regarding your circumstances and your real position?" Guérin knew that time did not lend itself well to long episodes of correspondence, and Mother Mary was not in a position to judge events in Indiana. Even Mother Mary knew that, at one point writing, "it is difficult for us to judge from here what would be for the best there, but we are confident that you will be able to get along when you have the sufficient knowledge of the country in which you are living."

Guérin worried that the community would somehow become a separate entity from the motherhouse in Ruillé, and if that happened, she feared that the tiny community would only have Providence to rely on in order to survive. She expressed to Bishop Jean-Baptiste Bouvier in France that Bishop Hailandière was doing all he could for the congregation including having a great deal of work done on their house, but she was more interested in paying off the community's debts rather than spending money on things it did not need. She conveyed her difficulty with the unstable position she was in to her superiors in France and made sure that they realized how much she wished to remain an establishment of Ruillé. "I am not always of his opinion [Bishop Hailandière]; for instance, as to the reception of subjects, admission to the habit, and even to the vows, and the acceptance of establishments. I am afraid of proceeding too quickly, and the Bishop says that in this country nothing is done slowly," she wrote in a letter to Bishop Bouvier. "I tell you all this only as a prelude to a favor I am going to ask in the name of all your daughters of the Woods, whether French or American . . . never permit this poor little House of the Forest to be separated from its trunk. . . . I believe we are even more attached to our dear Ruillé, to our good Mothers, than when we were at a less distance from them; and this sincere attachment is readily shared by all our Sisters of the New World."

In twelve months the sisters not only experienced illness, doubt, hardship, conflict, and disappointment but also established a convent, a school, and a working farm. There were signs that their little establishment would grow thanks to their diligent effort, but Guérin knew that there would be more challenges in store for the community at Saint Mary-of-the-Woods, and that the challenges ahead would more than likely prove to be an uphill battle.

Celestine de la Hailandiére, bishop of Vincennes

Chapter 5

One Step Forward

Things were far from easy for the sisters when Mother Theodore Guérin decided to open schools in other parts of the state. Her own community was barely off the ground and there were already tensions between her, Father Stanislaus Buteux, the former priest in charge of the community, Bishop Celestine de la Hailandière, and even problems with her superiors in France. Still, she decided to honor her promise to send sisters to Jasper, a small German community in southern Indiana. The citizens of the community fired the bricks to build a church and a convent for a community of sisters. The school opened its doors on March 19, 1842, with Sister Marie Joseph Pardeillan and Sister Gabriella Moore installed to act as teachers to fifty students. Sister Saint Vincent Ferrer Gagé was appointed as the superior.

Fulfilling the order's mission that the sisters must always maintain a free school, Guérin saw the need to establish one called Nazareth for the poor children who lived in and around the village of Saint Mary-of-the-Woods. In October, Sister Mary Liguori Tiercin and Sister Augustine Graham were installed in a log cabin school in Saint Francisville, Illinois. The school boasted an enrollment of sixty and was located just twelve miles from Vincennes.

Guérin's confidence was bolstered also by the growing number of vocations. "We are now six professed Sisters, nine novices, and eight postulants," she wrote to Bishop Jean-Baptiste Bouvier of Le Mans. "The example of Sister St. Francis Xavier [le Fer de la Motte] is of great advantage in forming our young candidates to the religious life." She prided the newcomers' ability to devote themselves wholly to the community, and there seemed to be no shortage of demand for the sisters. The increased vocations made staffing the new schools possible as well as the expansion of those already in existence.

Mother Mary Lecor in Ruillé, France, still had her concerns, however. Recent misunderstandings had made her uneasy about the Indiana mission, and she wrote to Guérin demanding a complete account of the Indiana establishments. "In none of your letters is there mention of suffering or the extraordinary difficulties . . . you appeared to be as happy as our Sisters in France. . . . I order you, without anyone whatever, by the obedience which you owe us, to inform us of all that concerns you in general and in particular. I wish to know everything, my dear Theodore . . . I oblige you to tell me the whole truth, no matter from what quarter your sufferings and difficulties may proceed."

Mother Mary's letter troubled Guérin. It was bad enough that the community's work had been misrepresented by an unknown person, but the admonition stung Guérin. She immediately wrote a response to Mother Mary's letter, taking pains to meticulously detail life at the Woods. "I do not recall ever to have hidden from you knowingly any of our sufferings. . . . It is very true that our whole life is one of sacrifice. Who could doubt this? Strangers to the manners and customs, to the religious opinions and especially to the character of the people who surround us, lost in the deep solitudes of Indiana, buried alive as it were in this vast tomb, without doubt, humanly speaking, our life is miserable . . . but, my dear Mother, you know all that so well that you forewarned me of it all yourself before I ever came to America."

In her lengthy letter, Guérin chronicled every aspect of the sisters' lives. She told Mother Mary of her issues with Bishop Hailandière as well as Father Buteux. She discussed her financial concerns and gave a full inventory of their animals and equipment, a progress report on the health of the sisters, the status of the school and the children, and even the local news. She wanted desperately for Mother Mary to have an accurate picture of life in Indiana and to know that her daughters were doing all they could to establish a life in the American wilderness.

Guérin still had no answer as to whether or not she would be separated from the congregation in France. The dilemma prompted her to ask for advice from several of her colleagues. Many of the priests who had visited her saw her as an extraordinary woman who was destined to do a lot of good in the area. She turned to Father Napoleon J. Perché of New Orleans, who encouraged her to be bold and to write her superiors again, bluntly asking what was their intention regarding the congregation. "It is necessary to remain firm, my dear daughter," Father Perché wrote. "I know that the hardest trials are those which come to us from persons for whom we have esteem and respect."

Despite the internal issues regarding who was ultimately responsible for the congregation, the young community was doing well. While economic resources remained scarce, the congregation's crops had yielded enough produce to see them through the winter. The establishments outside Saint Mary-of-the-Woods were well received, and as the new school term began, many parents enrolled their children. Several of the families were non-Catholics, but they liked the idea of sending their children to a French academy regardless of its religious connotation.

But the good times were not to last. On October 2, 1842, Guérin was talking to one of her novices when the peaceful quiet was shattered by the cry of "Fire!" The entire community ran to the doors of the convent and saw two of its buildings awash in flames. While everyone rallied to bring buckets, Guérin realized that the roof of the farmhouse was already on fire and the wind was carrying sparks over to the adjacent barn. Immediately the sisters knew their little house was doomed, and there was a mad rush to save the contents of the barn, which contained the sisters' store of winter provisions. It was no use. The sisters who went into the barn were immediately driven out by the inferno. "In less than three minutes the two buildings containing our wagons, plows, and all the farm implements constituted an immense oven from which a bright and circling flame rose . . . and threw to a great distance a shower of sparks," Guérin wrote to Mother Mary the next day. "Carried by a brisk, though not high wind, the sparks kindled fires all around making the first one still more terrible."

The sisters and the workers watched in horror as the trees caught fire and a brisk wind threatened the convent. They wanted to cover the house with wet sheets, but the lack of a river or stream nearby made this impossible. Guérin knew prayer was her only ally at this point, and she left the scene of the blaze for a moment to go to the chapel in order to kneel before the Blessed Sacrament, praying that God might save her little house. When she returned, the men had begun chopping down trees in order to create a break in the path of the fire and to protect the convent. As the trees fell, the limbs landed on those who were working and burned their clothes and hair. Guérin, the sisters, and the men all sustained minor injuries. Luckily, no one was seriously injured.

As the wind died down, Guérin was able to assess the situation. The community had sustained serious losses, and any attempt to salvage what remained was futile because another strong wind would send the situation spiraling out of control once again. Guérin sent for some wine to dispense to the men who had worked so tirelessly to stop the blaze, and they watched rubble of the buildings burn long into the night. Finally Guérin was convinced the worst was over. All that was left were half-burned logs, collapsed beams, and ruined crops.

Naturally everyone was curious as to what caused the fire in the first place. Anti-Catholic feeling was prevalent in America, and it was not uncommon for an arsonist to burn a convent to the ground, leaving the sisters in these communities penniless and without a home or provisions. Guérin seemed convinced that the fire at Saint Mary's was the result of this prejudice, but there was never any proof that such an act took place. "It seems impossible that it could have happened otherwise," she wrote to Mother Mary. "The fire showed itself on the outside about seven feet above ground in a board of the gable of the farmhouse. The fence had been broken down on the side of the woods about twenty steps away. This must have been done during High Mass, and the fire started and covered up so that it did not break out until half an hour after midday."

Guérin was scared. Bishop Hailandière wrote to try to calm her fears while pointing out that he found her anxiety to be exaggerated. "Is it quite true that you are 'surrounded by enemies and without defense?' And why this complaint so often renewed, 'in the midst of a forest?' . . . I beg of you, my daughter, in your own interest and for my own consolation, do not write these things to me. Be calm, walk gently in the Presence of God. Have a little confidence in Him."

As fingers were pointed and blame was laid, Guérin knew only one thing for certain: everything the community had worked for was lost. As she made preparations to salvage whatever was left in order to survive the coming months, she wrote to Mother Mary, explaining their dire circumstances. "For meat we have killed some of our animals and have exchanged others for oats and corn . . . if we need butter, tallow, soap, etc., we are obliged to give in exchange sugar or coffee or cotton print or calico etc. . . . Our creditors, however, torment us like mad men. I have paid about a hundred dollars of the amount received from Monseigneur [Bishop Hailandière] and Mr. [Samuel] Byerley, but it is like a drop of oil on a fire. It only intensifies their thirst for money, and this money famine may cause our destruction in this country where we thought our Congregation was called to do so much good."

Friends and colleagues heard about the fire from Guérin's account and sent gifts of money and encouraging letters of support. Several offered alternative causes for the fire. Father Edward Sorin in South Bend did not corroborate the arson story, but rather congratulated Guérin on her faith in God and encouraged her to keep her confidence up. Mother Mary Cecilia Bailly wrote many years later that it was determined that careless workers smoking started the blaze, and Bishop Hailandière offered that John Marcile, the superintendent who was in charge of the work on the church, was responsible for the fire.

The aftereffects of the fire were far reaching, and as the winter months began, the sisters were frugal with their minimal resources and conserved what they had. Each day was a challenge as Guérin tried to stretch the meager resources among the sisters and the students. She unfortunately had to dismiss two of the farmhands because there were simply no funds with which to pay them.

Relations between Guérin and the bishop continued to deteriorate. Guérin was not permitted to visit her establishments because Bishop Hailandière felt that the schools and other facilities should rely on local priests for support. Yet the sisters at the other establishments longed to see their mother. Sister Saint Francis Xavier was practicing the strictest frugality while being admonished by the bishop for spending too much. Father Perché, a close confidant of Guérin's, sympathized, writing to her that he shared in her trials with the bishop and that for the time being she had to hold firm because it was her duty. He reminded her that no saint has an easy road.

The fire and subsequent power struggles were only the tip of the iceberg. The United States was also suffering an economic crisis.

Sister Saint Francis Xavier le Fer de la Motte

The value of the dollar had fallen, and the bank where the sisters deposited their money had folded. The winter was harsh, and as 1843 began, the sisters struggled. Bishop Bouvier sent one thousand francs to help them get by, but their financial outlook seemed so bleak that Guérin contemplated a journey to France in order to raise funds and perhaps finally to determine to whom the congregation belonged.

Given the amount of

debt the sisters were in, Guérin had a hard time justifying the trip abroad, but she knew that the circumstances warranted such a journey. The congregation could not wait for months for a reply to its letters to France, and the bishop had made it clear that he could not financially support the congregation's debts and projected expenses.

Bishop Hailandière left the final decision up to Guérin, although he did outline the pros and cons of the journey. He wanted her to go primarily to put to rest all of the negative reports that had been given to Mother Mary regarding the congregation. He also hoped that the superiors in France would provide the fledgling congregation with prayers, novices, and economic resources. Members of the community were concerned about who would replace Guérin in her absence and apprehensive about her undertaking such a strenuous journey with her poor health. The Sisters of Providence Council met in order to discuss the benefits of the journey. In the end, it was decided that she should go. The bishop approved of the voyage on April 26, 1843, and Guérin and Sister Mary Cecilia traveled to France aboard the *Sylvia*.

When they arrived in Ruillé, the two sisters discovered it was not a good time to ask for financial backing from France. Although Bishop Hailandière had given Guérin several letters and allowed her to use his name for the purposes of obtaining the funds they needed, she discovered that the Society for the Propagation of the Faith, a Catholic organization that helped missions with prayers and money, would do no more for them than it already was. Any money collected would have to come from private benefactors. Sadly, many people who might have been in a position to help her congregation were away from the city and letters of appeal had to be left with caretakers. In addition, France was in the midst of an economic downturn and continuous rain had destroyed crops, making the solicitation of funds difficult. Those who Guérin was able to visit did all they could to help her. She left no stone unturned as she put aside her ill health and fatigue to solicit funds for her mission. However, her efforts barely secured enough money to pay for her passage back to America.

She also used the trip to obtain answers from Mother Mary and her superiors in Ruillé regarding to whom the Indiana congregation belonged and what was expected of them. During a meeting in September 1843 with Mother Mary, the Sisters of Providence Council and Bishop Bouvier, she discovered that the congregation of Saint Mary-of-the-Woods was a self-governing foundation from that of Ruillé, and its superior authority was the bishop of Vincennes. Guérin also learned that she could expect nothing from the motherhouse in Ruillé except benevolence and charity. The motherhouse agreed that per the original agreement, if the six sisters who were sent from France to Indiana ever wanted to return to Ruillé, they would be allowed to return, but the congregation of Ruillé did not have the right to recall the sisters without the consent of the bishop of Vincennes. Guérin wondered if the congregation at Ruillé would pay the travel expenses of a sister who wanted to return to France, and she was told that the sisters should write to the superiors in France and wait for a response.

Guérin wanted to determine if the sisters were sent to Indiana in order to establish a congregation based on Ruillé or if they were sent to establish a congregation based on the wants of the bishop of Vincennes. She was told that the Indiana congregation was to be based on that of Ruillé in every way possible. The goal for everyone involved was to maintain the same constitution and rules for both congregations. The motherhouse encouraged communication between the Indiana congregation and the bishop of Vincennes, but if the bishop gave an order, the sisters were to obey until such time that the matter could be formally discussed between the superior (in this case Guérin) and the bishop of Vincennes. Guérin also learned that the Saint Mary-of-the-Woods congregation of the Sisters of Providence was the only one that could admit a postulant or novice to the community. The bishop of Vincennes certainly had the right to present someone to the council or to veto the subject, but the council must be included in admitting new members of the community. The bishop had the authority to place and to displace the sisters in the different employments in the congregation, but if he forbade the visitation of new missions, Guérin was told she should visit them anyway.

The meeting served to confirm the actions Guérin had taken with the bishop of Vincennes. However, it also confirmed her suspicion that her congregation was separate from her beloved Ruillé. Although she wanted to see the congregations united as one, she knew that it was unrealistic. As Mother Mary wrote to Bishop Bouvier: "The superior general of Ruillé [Mother Mary] cannot be charged with the responsibility of a Congregation two thousand leagues from her residence; she cannot supervise the sisters, take part in the admission of subjects, nor their dismissal, nor in the acceptance of establishments or their refusal, etc. It would be necessary to depend on what was written to her, exact or inexact, true or false."

After the meeting, Guérin wrote to the sisters in Indiana to tell them of what transpired in France. She then resumed her quest for funds. When it became obvious that she might have to remain in France for the duration of the winter if she was to be successful at all, she knew the sisters back in America could not wait that long. They had dire needs of their own. Bishop Bouvier was confident he could arrange for free passage back to America and the Propagation of the Faith would provide assistance in the future. He did not feel that Guérin's absence was a good idea and believed she needed to return to Indiana as soon as possible.

Unfortunately, he was not able to secure their passage, and

Guérin resigned herself to writing to benefactors in order to gain fare to return to America. Disheartened, she was ready to give up when she humored Sister Mary Cecilia's request to send one more letter. "As I had several times refused Sister's request, I granted it this time, but it was only out of pure complaisance that I did so," Guérin wrote in her journal.

She presented herself to Mademoiselle Labrouche, who was the governess to the children of Martin du Nord, the keeper of the seals, minister of justice and of religious worship in Paris. Labrouche spoke to the minister on the sisters' behalf, and when he granted them an audience, he told Guérin that she should write directly to Marie Amalie, the queen of France and niece of Marie Antoinette. "We did so, and the Keeper of the Seals not only took the letter himself to St. Cloud, but, not being able to deliver it to the Queen, he gave it to the King and begged His Majesty to be our advocate with his royal consort," she wrote. While the king, Louis Philippe, was known for being a frugal man, the queen had a reputation for her generosity. She was born an Italian princess, and out of the half million francs allotted to her each year from her own family, she spent four hundred thousand of it on charity.

The audience with the queen took place on October 2, 1843, Guérin's forty-fifth birthday. When Marie Amalie entered the room, she immediately put the sisters at ease, inquiring about their situation and listening intently as Guérin described the hardships that the Indiana community had endured. The queen was moved to tears by the story. Guérin later wrote in her journal that the queen was sympathetic to their plight and asked what she could do for the community. "We replied that as a signal favor, we begged of her to pay our passage. She immediately answered: 'Your passage shall be paid. How many are you?' 'Four,' we answered; which was indeed true, since we had two postulants."

That, however, was not the end of the queen's benevolence.

Knowing that the sisters would need additional funds when they returned to Indiana, she offered to solicit help from the king and their children. She was so moved by the prospect of helping the sisters that at one moment she exclaimed, "Ah, yes, Sisters, let us save souls!" "There was in her manner, her eyes, and above all in her voice so intimate a conviction of the price of a soul that my

Queen Marie Amalie of France

heart was touched by it, and is so even yet in recalling that incident to my mind," Guérin wrote.

The sisters felt better after leaving the queen, but they were still unsure if the money for their passage would be paid. The queen was taken aback by the cost of the voyage, but true to her word, she procured the money for the sisters. In addition, thanks to the queen's endorsement, the sisters found themselves welcome in several homes, earning support for their mission in Indiana. "A number of persons of every station have shown such interest, such a desire for the prosperity of our work, and so many prayers have been and are still being offered," Guérin wrote. "I doubt not but God will bless this dear little Congregation."

The queen also made good on her promise to send more help

to the sisters once they returned to Indiana. A year later, she sent the congregation fifteen hundred dollars, which included not only the royal family's gift but also funds she was able to solicit from those around her. The sisters were very blessed by this special benefactress.

However, all was not well in Indiana. Some of the sisters found the news of the Indiana congregation's separation from Ruillé disturbing. Sister Basilide Sénéschal expressed that she would feel as if she were in another community entirely. Other sisters expressed similar concerns. They knew that some modifications of the Rule would be necessary in a different country, and they were ready to accept changes if the essentials were retained. Without the guidance and support of Ruillé and Bishop Bouvier, they were concerned that their mission was on shaky ground.

As if the sisters' worries were not enough, Bishop Hailandière held an election for a new superior general in Guérin's absence, threatening her position as head of the congregation at Saint Mary-of-the-Woods. Bishop Bouvier admonished the bishop of Vincennes for holding this election as well as his leadership of the community, and Mother Mary encouraged Guérin to "Make haste, my dear Theodore, fly to Vincennes to mend the broken vessels, to watch over your flock. . . . If your voyage to France has been useful, your presence at home is still more necessary."

Guérin and the sisters left France on November 28, 1843, taking a southern route across the Atlantic that passed through the Bahamas and other islands off the Atlantic coast, as winter was close at hand and the seas were rough. Writing to Bishop Bouvier from the Mississsppi River, Guérin said, "That painful voyage which lasted eight weeks is over, that voyage during which we had forty days of tempests, one in particular being most frightful. Never had the sailors seen the like, they said, and I easily believe it. During six days it only diminished a little from time to time to begin again with renewed fury." While on a stopover in New Orleans, Guérin fell ill. Because her convalescence required more than a few days' rest, she sent her companions on to Indiana without her. As she rested at an Ursuline convent, there was a storm brewing in Indiana. The bishop of Vincennes was continuing to run the congregation and exercise his will over the sisters.

Bishop Hailandière, Guérin informed Bishop Bouvier, had "formed two new establishments, withdrawn the Sisters from one which we had, given the habit to two postulants, admitted two novices to their vows, and received three Sisters from another Community—all without the advice or consent of the Sisters. They tried to make representations but he answered that he had foreseen their objections and would be obeyed."

Her health was now the least of her worries. Guérin knew she had to return to Saint Mary-of-the-Woods. Indiana was no longer the "land of exile," but her home. In it, Guérin wrote, "I hope to dwell all the days of my life."

Father John Corbe

Chapter 6

A Belief in Providence

It is very hard to maintain a good working relationship when
tensions between employer and employee grow increasingly
strained. In the case of Bishop Celestine de la Hailandière and
Mother Theodore Guérin, their individual visions for the
congregation frequently conflicted and the turmoil that ensued
caused many problems within the community. Until her journey
to France proved otherwise, Guérin saw the congregation at
Saint Mary-of-the-Woods as an extension of the community of
Ruillé. Bishop Hailandière believed the sisters to be a diocesan
congregation and subject to the will of the bishop of Vincennes.
The bishop was proud of what the sisters had accomplished, and

he often spent time at Saint Mary-of-the-Woods when he needed moments of tranquility and solitude. He also invested many of his own monetary resources in the community, even to the point of his own discomfort. Unfortunately, the bishop lacked the skills necessary to run a productive diocese.

During the sisters' first year in America the bishop was content to let them live according to the Rule and constitution of their order. However, in the congregation's second year Bishop Hailandière began to resent the sisters. It was not uncommon for French priests to have difficulty relating to women, but several in the area were doing all they could to foster friendships with these vital members of the diocese, including Father John Corbe, Father Anthony Parret, and Father Julian Benoit. Saint Mary's was not the only establishment that the bishop was having difficulty with. Bishop Hailandière had a power struggle with Father Edward Sorin, the founder of Notre Dame, as well. He tried to prevent Sorin from working with several other dioceses and sought control over the acquisition of Old Saint Mary's College near Lebanon, Kentucky. The bishop's battles with Sorin mirrored his issues with Guérin to some degree, centering on his belief that he was in complete control of the diocese and that all religious and clergy were subject to compliance.

In some ways, the bishop was aware of his shortcomings as an administrator. When Guérin traveled to France, he wrote to Father Corbe, who had replaced Father Stanislaus Buteux as chaplain, and said that he "would not be surprised if within six weeks this house would be in a turmoil." In 1845 he appealed to Rome to accept his resignation as the bishop of Vincennes, but Pope Gregory XVI rejected his appeal. Although he had the best of intentions, every aspect of religious life that he was involved in seemed to go awry. Novices that he trained suddenly gave up on the religious life, sisters that he chose to assist sometimes experienced a crisis of faith, and other novices that he recruited "showed a spirit which made it hazardous to keep them yet they had to be retained for months through fear of incurring his displeasure."

Guérin understood that it was Bishop Hailandière's nature to interfere with the inner workings of the congregation and that he gave little regard for the rules adopted by the order, and she knew the day was coming when she would have to stand up to his interference. Although she bowed to his wishes many times, deferring to his role as bishop, some of his actions were questionable. At one point he convinced four Sisters of Charity to leave their order and be admitted into the Sisters of Providence without going through a proper novitiate. At the mission of Vincennes, Bishop Hailandière chose postulants as teachers rather than experienced teachers who were readily available. That decision alone nearly ran the school into ruin. Guérin kept her congregation together through tact and diplomacy. She knew that leaving the diocese for Europe, even for a short time, would be risky.

Bishop Hailandière's anger was not geared to the community as a whole but focused on Guérin and Sister Saint Francis Xavier le Fer de la Motte, and he wanted both of them gone. Pursued by creditors and unrest in the diocese, he spent a month at Saint Mary's early in 1844, while Guérin was in France. He was able to keep an eye on her, thanks to his correspondents, as she moved about France. Even though he was aware of her early fund-raising failures as well as her success in Paris, he repeatedly told Sister Basilide Sénéschal that Guérin would not return until spring, assuming that she would not be able to procure necessary funds until then.

His plan was to prevent Guérin from returning to Saint Mary-of-the-Woods at all. In her absence, he took over the duties of superior, exercising his will and control over the sisters. The sisters were afraid to move even a piece of furniture without his permission.

The bishop immediately contradicted any plan that Guérin put into place, creating an aura of distrust in the community. When he presented any dilemma to the sisters, they often felt that they had to choose between the two.

After declaring that he would not allow Guérin to return to Saint Mary's, he appointed Sister Basilide superior general. Sister Basilide knew she did not possess the qualifications to run the community, and she suspected that the bishop knew it, too, but merely wanted to gain a stronghold over the community. In 1843 Sister Basilide wrote to a former superior general in Ruillé that "there are too many difficulties here with this good Bishop who rules on everything according to his views . . . he has the best intentions in the world, but no one can convince him that things are otherwise than as he believes."

Guérin first learned about the bishop's plan when she returned from France and stopped in Vincennes to see Sister Saint Vincent Ferrer Gagé. The following day in a meeting with the bishop she was accused and charged with crimes she could hardly imagine. "He began to reproach me with the gravest and bitterest reproaches about things which I heard in astonishment," she recorded in her journal. "For not only did he relate to me under the blackest colors all that I had in the past said and proposed to the Council, but also a number of things that I had never thought of. . . . Among the countless accusations heaped upon me, one was that I was not sick at all in New Orleans, but had remained there to plot something against my superior."

Surprisingly, the bishop allowed Guérin to return to Saint Mary's even though he had repeatedly said that he would never allow it. Many believe that a letter from Father Corbe was responsible for the bishop's change of heart. Father Corbe felt the bishop's actions were too harsh and, given the state of the diocese, he decided to speak out rather than keep the peace at any cost. Whatever the intervention, Guérin was back home, where an uneasy peace reigned. She repaid all of her debts with the money she had received from France and jumped back into the work around the convent, making repairs and helping with the never-ending farmwork. She also oversaw the construction of a log cabin that was dedicated in honor of Saint Anne, the patron saint of Brittany, France. Guérin felt that a structure in honor of Saint Anne was appropriate since she had prayed through the saint for a safe journey during her long voyage back from France, particularly when the weather was stormy. (The cabin was replaced in 1876 with a newer structure, now known as the Saint Anne Shell Chapel.)

The sisters at the missions were desperate for Guérin to visit them, but she feared doing so would upset the bishop. She was

Saint Anne Shell Chapel

caught in a dilemma between stepping on the bishop's toes and remaining faithful to the order's Rule, which stated that she must visit her establishments. Eventually, at Father Corbe's request, Guérin traveled to Vincennes to confer with the bishop. "He could not have been more friendly," she wrote to Bishop Jean-Baptiste Bouvier of Le Mans in June 1844. "He wished again to make excuses to me. I assured him that that was not necessary, that very candidly I had forgotten the past." Guérin requested permission to continue following the Rule of her order within the diocese. The bishop said he saw the wisdom in the Rule and felt it should be followed as it was in France, with one exception. He still wanted to retain control over the foundation of new establishments.

During the course of their discussion, the bishop told Guérin that he had every intention of giving the sisters the title to the land that Saint Mary's was on. Though he had sold a portion of it, he wanted to return the deed to the sisters. Once the sisters had returned his investment, the land would be theirs, and the bishop would no longer financially support them. The sisters could not have been happier. Guérin was hardly worried about the lack of funds from the bishop. Writing to Bishop Bouvier, she said, "Poverty did not affright us."

Her happiness, however, soon waned. Weeks passed and the bishop did not procure the deed to the land. The sisters were once again at the bishop's mercy. Although he claimed he wanted nothing to do with the affairs of the sisters, he could not remain uninvolved, whether it was in the creation of new establishments, the repairs to existing ones, or ordering Father Corbe to sell the bricks that had been made earlier in the spring to add wings to the expanding boarding school.

The bishop's flagrant abuse of power was more than Guérin could bear. Not only did Bishop Hailandière create tension within Guérin's congregation, he also spent time discrediting the community to other priests within the diocese. It seemed that every time the bishop exercised his power, Guérin lost a little of her own. He seemed content to make the fulfillment of their Rule impossible, and in a moment of frustration, she wrote to Bishop Bouvier saying, "What do you wish us to do? Remain here? In that case we must resign ourselves to not being able to fulfill our Rules. . . . Should we return to France? But in that case, what shall we do with these poor girls who have left all that was dear to them in the world to come and ask us to lead them to God? . . . I beg you not to abandon us, we have only you for refuge. Have pity on your poor daughters of the woods."

Guérin came to the conclusion that if the bishop was going to disregard their Rule entirely, it might be time to start over somewhere outside of the Vincennes diocese. She hinted to such a plan in a letter to Sister Saint Vincent Ferrer in 1844. Unfortunately, the bishop intercepted the letter. Offended, his grip on the community tightened further. It was characteristic of Bishop Hailandière to act dramatically when it came to the sisters. One case in particular involved the Vincennes school. Although Guérin believed the schools were her responsibility, he rerouted to the Vincennes school a couple of boarding students who were originally headed to Saint Mary's. When she challenged him on his decision, the bishop became so enraged that he dropped his role as the ecclesiastical superior of the Sisters of Providence.

Father Corbe, who Guérin considered to be a blessing to the congregation, became his replacement. Father Corbe was a good friend of the bishop and was able to appeal to the bishop's softer side on delicate issues. Guérin hoped he would be able to help her reach a peaceful agreement with the bishop. Unfortunately, Father Corbe could not get any further with the bishop than she did. In fact, Bishop Hailandière was angry that she sent Father

Corbe to talk to him at all. The bishop wrote to Father Corbe and told him that he had asked Guérin, "in what do I oppose your following your Rule, I who never interfere in your affairs? What have I regulated or commanded contrary to your Constitutions? I oppose your Rules! Rest assured, that will be so no longer. For I have asked Father Corbe to be my delegate . . . he will be your local superior."

Even though he appointed Father Corbe as his replacement, the bishop remained unwilling to give up the smallest amount of control. Knowing that she might leave the diocese altogether, Bishop Hailandière instructed Father Corbe to make sure no sister traveled without his permission, especially Guérin. "I positively forbid that any sister be sent or remain all alone in an establishment, that anyone travel alone without a special permission from you or from me. Let none of them go out of the diocese," he wrote. "As for the mother, I am opposed to her visiting her establishments without a written permission from the bishop, or in my absence from the diocese, you alone."

Without the bishop's support, the congregation would fail. Guérin began to look for opportunities for the sisters to move their mission outside of the diocese and away from Bishop Hailandière. Writing to Bishop Bouvier again, she told him that their boarding school was in need of repairs, and in the bishop's absence Father Corbe had given permission for the necessary repairs to be made. When Bishop Hailandière arrived to oversee the work, the permissions granted did not meet with his approval. He dictated that any needed improvements would have to be made at the sisters' expense.

"We felt we should propose it to our sisters, but all unanimously refused to give their approval to this enterprise," she wrote to Bishop Bouvier in December of 1844. She told him that for the sisters to invest twenty thousand francs in this project on land that didn't belong to them in the first place was a poor idea. She also included that if the sisters did use their own money, they would still have to make the improvements according to Bishop Hailandière's specifications. She said that the sisters did not even have the freedom at the current time to make any adjustments to the building including the seemingly simple repair of putting a banister on a stairway where children were in danger of getting hurt.

When Bishop Hailandière arrived to bless the church in the village of Saint Mary's, Guérin arranged to speak with him. She felt it was impossible to remain in a diocese where the sisters were on bad terms with the bishop, that it would be poor stewardship to build on land that still did not belong to them, and that the sisters could not remain in a place where they were not permitted to live according to the sacred rules and obligations that they understood to be part of their vocation. The bishop tersely responded that the congregation was his and always would be, and that Guérin was free to leave alone if she wanted to. Finally, he forbade her from setting foot in her own house again.

Guérin wanted a peaceful resolution to her difficulties with the bishop because she was finally beginning to see a lessening of the anti-Catholic prejudices in the area. Madison was a fine example of this change of attitude. In August 1844 Guérin entered into an agreement with Father Julian Delaune, who agreed to provide housing, a stipend, and funding to return the sisters from Madison to Saint Mary-of-the-Woods for their annual summer retreat. With money a constant issue, Father Delaune's offer was a terrific opportunity for the sisters to receive some of the financial resources they so desperately needed.

Madison, however, was home to a fairly large anti-Catholic population, and when the sisters opened their academy, there were only five Catholic students among the numerous Protestants that enrolled. Those students had been told every negative fact possible about the Catholic religion, and the sisters were subject to ridicule, were spat at on the street, and were insulted. Yet the sisters remained devoted to the academy, and eventually that dedication paid off as the tone of intolerance died down. "The most bigoted, the most prejudiced against them have already been appeased; two have even sent them their daughters. These children lose their prejudices in our schools, then the parents are won over," Guérin wrote.

Despite her desire to stay in the Vincennes diocese, Guérin did begin to look outside the diocese in case she needed to relocate the congregation. She knew she would not be the first person to leave the diocese due to disagreements with the bishop. After Bishop Hailandière left for Europe on November 18, 1844, Guérin contacted Bishop Peter Paul Lefevre of the Detroit diocese in Michigan, through French Canadian priest Father William Chartier in June of 1845, looking for a place to move the congregation. Bishop Lefevre told Guérin that he would love to have the Sisters of Providence as part of the Detroit diocese, and the two made plans for her relocation in the event that no settlement between her and Bishop Hailandière could be reached.

Bishop Hailandière was troubled by the turmoil in the Vincennes diocese, and although he did not stop in Ruillé to see Mother Mary Lecor while he was in France, he did visit with Bishop Bouvier of Le Mans. Bishop Bouvier encouraged him to allow the sisters to practice their Rule and to hand over the deed to the land that he promised them. To Bishop Hailandière's chagrin, he discovered that Guérin's confidant all of this time had been the bishop of Le Mans and not Mother Mary as he had suspected. He told Bishop Bouvier that he was wrong to offer Guérin advice on a diocese that was so far from his own and that he felt it was better for the sisters to rent their property rather than own it outright. He also accused Bishop Bouvier of overstepping his boundaries by giving orders to the sisters. Bishop Bouvier responded that he had only given advice and counsel. Incensed, Bishop Hailandière wrote Guérin from Rennes telling her that he had talked to Bishop Bouvier and that the bishop of Le Mans was far from pleased with her actions as well. He admonished her for wanting to move to a new location and he told her that she would have been better off if she would have listened to him all along. "All went well when you had confidence in your Bishop. It has been otherwise only from the moment that you took advice elsewhere."

Guérin was appalled by the misrepresentations that were made in Bishop Hailandière's letter. She was especially hurt by the implication that Bishop Bouvier was unhappy with her, and she immediately sent a letter to Le Mans to set the record straight. Bishop Bouvier replied that he was not displeased with Guérin and that "if absolutely you cannot remain, you know that Ruillé is disposed to receive again the Sisters it has given . . . nor would we object if at your own risk you should go to establish yourselves elsewhere. When you left us so courageously for America, you did not foresee the trials which awaited you there." Bishop Hailandière was determined that Bishop Bouvier would not continue to advise the sisters and informed the bishop of Le Mans that since his authority did not extend to Vincennes the sisters would not recognize any order that Bishop Bouvier sent. Bishop Hailandière's belligerence caused Bishop Bouvier to write, "You see, my dear Sister, that I can do nothing further for you."

By the winter of 1845, when her troubles with the bishop reached a climax, the only thing keeping Guérin together was a belief in Providence. Although she had again fallen ill, she composed a resignation letter to Bishop Hailandière, stating that "I find that it is time to come to an end. One word only, it will be the last. . . . I proposed to you many times that I abandon this dear Congregation that I love so much and for which I asked God to let me continue to live, not exacting, not asking anything of you except that you adopt, that you protect this Congregation, that you approve the Rules. . . . I have done all that I could to avoid this misfortune, for I love Indiana with my whole soul. To do good there, to see our Congregation solidly established there before I die, was my whole ambition; the good God has permitted that you did not wish it; may his will be done."

Members of the order's council also sent a letter to the bishop asking him to make good on his promises. "Many times you have said, and even written, that you intended to grant us these things, but that we had put obstacles. These obstacles are now removed—all the Sisters of Providence can now hold property legally; therefore, we dare hope that you will not delay to give us this last proof of your good will, which, in putting an end to a state so painful for all, will open to our view a brighter future," the sisters wrote.

The bishop became enraged and demanded that the sisters provide him with an apology letter. He accused them of speaking against him to his superiors in France and demanded that they present him with an immediate retraction. Given his power in the diocese, the sisters felt that they had no choice but to sign it. Afterwards he pardoned nearly all of the sisters except Guérin, whom he felt had betrayed him beyond consolation. In an act of generosity, he promised the sisters the deed to Saint Mary-of-the-Woods and the adoption of the rules of their order. The catch, of course, was that they promise to remain in the diocese.

The congregation hoped that Bishop Hailandière would act in good faith. However, his inconsistent behavior continued. He tried to force Guérin to write a request to return to France. When that failed, he presented the congregation with the deed to the land, but it only amounted to about eighty acres. He kept the remaining portion of the property as well as his controlling interest so that the sisters could not make any improvements on their portion without his approval and consent. Guérin expressed her concerns about the deed's legitimacy to Bishop Bouvier, saying, "it is probable that the deed will not be valid, I took it to a lawyer who will examine it and tell us whether it is legal or not. I tremble lest it be badly drawn."

Aside from the tension between Guérin and Bishop Hailandière, the academy and the establishments in Madison, Vincennes, Jasper, Montgomery, and Saint Francisville, Illinois, were doing well. Capital was always an issue, but Guérin was pleased with enrollment and was able to put some money aside that would help open a new academy in Fort Wayne. However, the fragile calm that existed between the community and the bishop was shattered when the bishop attempted to hold a secret election for superior just after the sisters' annual retreat in 1846.

The sisters were not about to betray Guérin and wrote to Father Corbe asking his counsel. He advised them to tell the bishop that there was only one candidate for the position and that she must be automatically elected. When the bishop heard this, he accused the sisters once again of thwarting his authority. As they pleaded with him to see reason, he ignored their cries and refused to associate with them. He even renounced them as a religious community, taking away from them whatever little power they possessed.

In the spring of 1847 Guérin visited her establishments throughout the diocese, acting as though nothing was wrong as she checked on everyone's progress and wrote to her sisters about her travels. She and the sisters who were accompanying her on her journey planned to see the bishop while passing through Vincennes on their way home to Saint Mary's. Just before her arrival, Guérin received a message from Father Corbe telling her not to enter into any negotiations with Bishop Hailandière and to place her faith in the community should the discussion of elections arise. "You can extricate yourself by simply telling him that if the Community wishes it you will not oppose it. If he tries to force you to give in your resignation, or makes any other proposals for you to sign, excuse yourself by leaving everything to the decision of the Community," Father Corbe advised.

Guérin was nervous when she visited Bishop Hailandière on May 20, 1847. The bishop's stubborn nature and demand for control dominated the conversation, as the bishop accused her of wanting to be superior to him. Realizing that the best defense was a good offense, Guérin offered to hold an election of the community, in which she would be willing to take their judgment as law. If they demanded her removal, she would resign from her post immediately.

The bishop, however, was not in the mood to negotiate. For what felt like hours, he reproached her and told her to give in to his demands. When she did not he insisted that she remain in Vincennes until she was prepared to give in to all of his requirements. Leaving the reception room to go down to dinner, he locked Guérin inside. The sisters who she was staying with became concerned and went to the bishop to find their superior. He took them to the door and unlocked it, where they found Guérin on her knees asking for the bishop's blessing. He blessed her and then motioned her out.

Later that evening, the bishop came to the Sisters of Providence residence in Vincennes, where he pronounced his final judgment on Guérin. "The Bishop declared to our Mother that not only was she no longer the Superior but that she was not now even a Sister of Providence, for he released her from her vows; that she had to leave the diocese immediately and go elsewhere to hide her disgrace; that he forbade her to write to the Sisters at Saint Mary's—they had no need of her letters," wrote Sister Saint Francis Xavier in her report to Archbishop Samuel Eccleston of Baltimore. In one swift move Guérin was dismissed from her congregation and forbidden to return to Saint Mary's or to communicate with the sisters.

When the congregation learned of what had transpired, they immediately prepared to leave home as well as to find Guérin and to go wherever she led. As they rallied to her defense, the bishop made it clear that anyone who left the diocese would be excommunicated. He threatened to send the law after anyone who took anything that he felt belonged to him. None of the sisters were surprised at the threat, and they vowed to face an uncertain future if it meant that they would be reunited with Guérin.

The sisters rallied the support of the workers and the gardeners at Saint Mary-of-the-Woods who were willing to leave the premises for the sake of Guérin. The sisters wrote to Guérin, and although she took comfort in their words of encouragement, she feared for their safety and the ramifications if they followed through with their resolution. In addition to sending a report to the bishop of Baltimore, the sisters wrote to the superiors in France telling them all that transpired, yet all they could do was to put their faith in Providence alone.

On May 25, 1847, the sisters received word that Guérin was ill. They immediately made plans to smuggle her back to Terre Haute so they could take care of her, but she did not want to go against the will of the bishop and did not wish to get the congregation in any more trouble. Sister Olympiade Boyer and Sister Mary Cecilia Bailly traveled to Vincennes to take care of her while the rest of the sisters continued preparations to leave the diocese. Father Corbe, who was furious at the turn of events, resigned, which baffled Bishop Hailandière, who believed that the problems were between the bishop and the congregation alone. The sisters repeatedly wrote to the bishop, trying to get him to reconsider his position, but their pleas fell on deaf ears. The bishop returned their letters to them unopened.

Just when it seemed that all hope was lost, Providence intervened. Bishop Hailandière received word from Rome that his resignation had finally been accepted. A new bishop, John Stephen Bazin, was assigned to the Vincennes diocese. Bishop Hailandière appointed Father Corbe to be the overseer for the Sisters of Providence, and he immediately sent for Guérin. The sisters and the townspeople came out to welcome her when she arrived from Vincennes on the steamboat *Daniel Boone* on June 10, 1847.

After her return, Guérin heard rumors that Bishop Hailandière was planning to remain in the diocese until Bishop Bazin got settled. Guérin was terribly worried about how much influence Bishop Hailandière might have on the new bishop. She wrote to Bishop Bouvier asking him to intervene with Bishop Bazin so that he would look favorably on the order and prove to be a welcome resource for the community. Bishop Bouvier had already corresponded with the new bishop, and he was pleased to inform Guérin that Bishop Bazin did not harbor any ill feelings toward the sisters and was looking forward to working with them. He merely wanted them to continue with their work in the diocese according to their rules.

John Stephen Bazin, bishop of Vincennes

Chapter 7

The Fresh Start

When John Stephen Bazin succeeded Bishop Celestine de la Hailandière as the bishop of Vincennes on October 24, 1847, it was as if a quiet peace settled over the congregation at Saint Mary-of-the-Woods. The new bishop won the hearts of everyone he came in contact with at Vincennes, including Sister Saint Francis Xavier le Fer de la Motte and Sister Marie Joseph Pardeillan. Sister Marie Joseph wrote a glowing report to Mother Theodore Guérin: "When I saw the Bishop for the first time today enter the sanctuary in his pontifical robes, I felt my heart fill with love and gratitude toward God. I feel sure that you will like him."

The new bishop was very anxious to meet Guérin and invited her to Vincennes in order to discuss future endeavors for the sisters. Once again Guérin was recovering from a difficult illness, and her physicians warned her not to rush a journey. Although she was still weak, she wanted to go to Vincennes and meet the man she had heard so much about. To her delight, the bishop was everything she could have wanted and more. He showed a great deal of kindness toward her and listened sympathetically as she told him about the sisters' recent struggles. Guérin came away from this meeting very satisfied. The bishop reminded her of Bishop Jean-Baptiste Bouvier of Le Mans, for whom she always had considerable respect.

Although Bishop Hailandière approved the Rule of the order before he left office, he never settled matters regarding the title deed at Saint Mary-of-the-Woods. Bishop Bazin wasted no time transferring the deed. Once she acquired the deed, Guérin was able to begin making the improvements that she had planned for her property. Even though she was fifty and beginning to feel her age, Guérin did not let her age or poor health stop her from continuing her work. She entered into each endeavor with the zeal and enthusiasm of a much younger woman.

Her letters during this time are a testament to the enthusiasm she was feeling about her vocation. It is hard to believe that during this period of intense activity that she had a bout with pneumonia and had to sustain herself on a diet of gruel and, occasionally, seasoned squirrel broth. As each new season brought changes in the congregation, she never missed an opportunity to tell her colleagues and superiors about the wondrous opportunities there were to serve in the diocese and to become a staple in the growing community.

Of course it helped that Bishop Bazin was enthusiastic about the sisters' work. He and Guérin entered into several projects together, one of which was a free pharmacy in Vincennes. Bazin had realized that many in the local community who were poor and sick also suffered from neglect and wanted to do something to help improve their health. Guérin was eager to help him with this effort. She immediately suggested Sister Olympiade Boyer for the job even though she had never been separated from her sisters at the Woods. Sister Olympiade was a natural choice because of her nursing skills. Her careful nursing had helped Guérin recover from illness more than once. Sister Olympiade had an abundance of natural remedies at her disposal. Mullein, pokeroot, calomel, mint, and horehound were easily found in the woods, and she also had seasonal cures such as pennyroyal, elder blossom, and sassafras root. On March 22, 1848, she left for Vincennes with Guérin and Sister Joachim Bodin.

Guérin also was able to begin working on building additions and landscaping projects, which had been put off until the land deed was settled. These additions enhanced the beauty of the grounds and expanded accommodations at the academy. The improvements to the grounds and a good harvest created an optimistic outlook in the community. Unfortunately, this prosperity did not last.

In 1848 Guérin and Sister Mary Cecilia Bailly traveled to Vincennes to participate in Holy Week services and to tour the houses in the various establishments. There they learned that Bishop Bazin was very ill and had taken to bed on Palm Sunday. Writing to Sister Saint Francis Xavier, Guérin told her that the bishop apparently had been ill since the beginning of Lent. "This, however, did not prevent him from preaching in his turn and in that of Father [Ernest] Audran, who is not strong . . . on Saturday, he spent six consecutive hours in the confessional. While there he was taken with a violent fever which obliged him to go to bed . . . everybody finds him in a serious condition. Pray much for him. It would be an immense loss if he should die."

Guérin went immediately to minister to the bishop, and on Holy Saturday she was called in to bleed him. She realized that the bishop was very near death, and she wrote to the sisters telling them that she had "no more hope of saving him." Bishop Bazin died of pneumonia on Easter Sunday, 1848, ending his promising reign over the diocese. Guérin wrote the sisters announcing the bishop's death and assuring them that his thoughts were always with them.

Father Simon Lalumiere

SISTERS OF PROVIDENCE

102

"You will hardly believe the sad news that I must announce to you . . . he is dead . . . our dear and venerated Father, our Bishop, John Stephen Bazin . . . he gave us for you his last blessing . . . had you been here . . . you would have been touched at the burning words that came from his loving and charitable heart."

She told the sisters that during his eight-day illness, the bishop spoke of the sisters every day, assuring Guérin of his love for the congregation. Even at the hour of his death, he told her that if he had lived longer, he would not have spared any sacrifice for the prosperity of the congregation. In reassuring the sisters of the bishop's love for them, she challenged the sisters to remember his lasting legacy. "Let us never forget that if we wish to die like the Saints we must live like them. Let us force ourselves to imitate their virtues, in particular humility and charity, of which virtues . . . we shall be recognized as the daughters of this holy prelate, who was so humble and so filled with love for his brethren." In spite of her words to the community, Guérin was concerned that in light of their loss, the community would suffer. She was further distressed by rumors that Bishop Hailandière might return to the diocese. Something always seemed to be waiting to test the sisters' spirit.

After the burial of Bishop Bazin, Guérin traveled to Madison to oversee the construction of a school. Saint Vincent Academy was a joint project with Father Simon Lalumiere of Saint Joseph Church in Terre Haute. Father Lalumiere secured the site for the institution and the sisters were responsible for building and operating the facility, requiring the order to borrow money. Guérin was unsure about borrowing money for this institution, but she knew her reliance on Providence would see to its success.

Over the summer of 1848, Guérin decided to hold an election during the sisters' annual summer retreat. Although the congregation had never had an election before, Guérin thought it was wise because of the amount of growth the community had experienced. In her letter circular to the sisters dated June 14, 1848, she said, "It is time to begin to organize ourselves, as much as possible, according to our Rules and Constitutions. My duties have multiplied to such an extent that it is impossible for me to fulfill them. I feel deeply the need of sharing a burden which I can no longer carry alone." She proposed that the community elect a first assistant and a mistress of novices. She asked the sisters to choose wisely, as these two positions would highly affect the future success of the order. Anyone who made their vows during the 1845 retreat or before was eligible. The sisters chose Sister Mary Cecilia as the first assistant and Sister Saint Francis Xavier as the mistress of novices.

Following the retreat, the sisters turned their attention to the work at home in Terre Haute. The planned renovations had been besieged by delays, and as usual, the Indiana winter did nothing to expedite renovations. At one point, the Wabash River flooded, leaving the sisters stranded from the rest of the community and postponing the work further. When work was able to continue, Guérin was a constant presence on the work site. In addition to offering encouragement to the workers, she also learned many of the skills associated with the construction of the new day school for girls.

But she was discouraged that things were not moving fast enough. The school opening that was scheduled for November was pushed back to January. Guérin wrote Bishop Bouvier that more than fifty students were enrolled in the school and opportunities for the sisters were everywhere. She had great hope for her establishment in Terre Haute, which she thought was due to experience a boom in upcoming years. "It is certain that the town of Terre Haute will become one of the largest in Indiana, on account of its location. They are already making railroads, canals, doing away with the obstructions in the Wabash which prevent the passage of steamboats, and so forth. They do here in one year what in the Old World would not be done in ten."

She had heard that there were plans for a hospital in Terre Haute, and it was rumored that the sisters would be in charge of it. Guérin was excited at the prospect but she knew running such a facility would require more sisters who understood how to operate a hospital, and she hoped that the motherhouse in Ruillé would be able to provide some.

In addition, Guérin was encouraged by the warm reception the sisters received in the many towns of the diocese. There was such a demand for them that they actually had to turn establishments down because they still had to maintain their own house, and there were not enough sisters ready to staff establishments elsewhere.

Eventually, a new successor to Bishop Bazin was named to the Vincennes diocese. Father Jacques M. Maurice Landes d' Aussac de Saint-Palais had worked in Indiana for twelve years, and Guérin felt he had done "incalculable good" in the area, building several churches. Communities in which he had lived felt an enormous sense of loss after he left. He had been a good friend to Guérin's congregation during its difficult years, and she felt that her community would be in good hands. "We find Bishop St. Palais' administration much resembling your own, which renders him still dearer to us. Far from destroying the Rule he will help us fulfill it exactly, for he is full of piety and has very good judgment," she wrote Bishop Bouvier.

Attendance for the consecration of the new bishop of Vincennes was low due to bad weather, flooding, and an outbreak of cholera. Only two bishops were able to be present after riding over rough roads that gave their wagons trouble en route to the ceremony. Guérin, however, was present on January 14, 1849, when Bishop Saint-Palais was installed. Guérin was not long in sharing the news of the occasion with Bishop Bouvier as well as her concerns for her sisters who may have been afflicted with cholera. The outbreak was wreaking havoc in towns such as Cincinnati, Saint Louis, and New Orleans. She reported to the bishop that in some of these cities, as many as 125 people died in a day. "When the weather becomes colder the disease diminishes, only to break out again with redoubled violence when it grows warmer. . . . I do not think it is in Indiana yet, but all are in extreme fear of it," she wrote.

Cholera is a disease caused through poor sanitation, and the 1849 outbreak was particularly violent. Local newspapers printed a variety of remedies including salt, quinine, and calomel. Bishop Saint-Palais, convinced that the disease would come to the low-lying areas near rivers, gave the sisters responsibility for caring for those afflicted in Vincennes. When the disease finally reached them, Guérin gave Bishop Bouvier complete details of the ravages the disease left in its wake. She had received word by telegraph that the losses due to disease were huge. On July 3 alone, 160 people had died in Saint Louis and another 127 had perished in Cincinnati. The schools in Madison had been closed, and several of the sisters were taking care of the sick in their homes, which was very dangerous to the sisters' health. "The plague has made its appearance at Indianapolis, Vincennes, Lafayette, Washington and several other localities; at Terre Haute, and even in the village at St. Mary's. For several weeks there has been sort of discomfort, colic, disordered stomach, dizziness. During the past few days all this has become more serious, *des cholérines*, as it is called here, *cholera morbus*, less dangerous

Jacques M. Maurice Landes d'Aussac de Saint-Palais, bishop of Vincennes

than malignant cholera, so called in English. The condition of the atmosphere tends to increase the fatal effects of the disease," Guérin wrote Bishop Bouvier.

Although her own diet was scant, Guérin encouraged the other sisters to be extra careful with cleanliness and to eat well during this time. She even suspended the traditional observances of Lent in order for the sisters to remain healthy. "I beseech you to be sure to write me at least three times a week, even if only a few lines, to let

SISTERS OF PROVIDENCE

106

me know how you are, whether the disease spreads, or whether it has disappeared,—in a word, *everything*," she wrote to the sisters at Madison. She went on to tell the sisters that "I have confidence, however, that God will not permit any of you to be attacked by the epidemic. Be cheerful, kind to one another. Have nothing on your conscience that could trouble you. Do not fast. Let your food be wholesome and well prepared. Keep your house, the yard, and also your persons clean. Change your linen often, and have your children clean also, if they are still with you. Finally, my dear daughters pray."

Eventually the cholera outbreak subsided, and Guérin began collaborating with her new prelate. When Bishop Saint-Palais had to close his seminary because of funding, Guérin took the responsibility for educating two students. It was the first time they worked with each other, but it would not be the last.

When Guérin set out in April 1849 on her yearly tour of the establishments, she came upon the children at the Fort Wayne establishment, many of whom were orphans of Miami Indian heritage. The children loved her, and she felt the same way about them, writing that she wished she could be a mother to all of the children who had lost their parents. Just like the foundress, Bishop Saint-Palais felt for the plight of the children of Indiana. When he heard about the number of children in Vincennes who were orphans he commissioned Guérin and the sisters to establish two new orphanages in Vincennes to minister to the children's needs. Although the bishop planned to include both boys and girls, he at first gave only the girls to the sisters' care, hoping to put the boys into the care of Father Edward Sorin. The first asylum opened on August 29, 1849.

When it came to taking on the care of boys, Guérin had her reservations. Aside from the Rule expressly stating that their care would be for girls, she knew boys tended to be more rambunctious and instruction of them would require great skill. This fact reinforced Guérin's reluctance to assume charge of the boys' orphan asylum, but by late 1850 the sisters were caring for thirty boys in addition to the forty-seven girls, not to mention overseeing the education of about six to seven hundred students throughout the state.

Guérin and the sisters were also offered a new establishment. This time the location was in Louisiana, far from home. While it would have been a great opportunity for the community, the proposition came with its own set of problems that had to be hammered out before it could be accepted. "The proposal of this establishment raised among us a slight contest, or, rather, a difference of opinion," Guérin wrote. The difference of opinion surrounded how this new establishment would be interpreted according to the Rule. On the one hand, Sister Saint Francis Xavier believed that the congregation could accept the establishment and send sisters to run it without first seeking the permission of the bishop of Vincennes, as long as the ecclesiastical superior, or local priest, approved. On the other hand, Guérin felt that the bishop had the sole authority to authorize the relocation of the sisters to a new establishment. When she sent a letter to Bishop Bouvier outlining the two conflicting opinions, he wrote back to assure her that the Rule was specific on this matter and that she was correct on the issue. In the end, the sisters did not accept the new opportunity.

During the summer of 1850, Bishop Saint-Palais joined the sisters during their annual retreat at the motherhouse in Saint Mary-of-the-Woods. After experiencing the cramped quarters and stifling August heat, the bishop decided that the sisters needed a new motherhouse and they needed it now. It was obvious that the ramshackle, two-story Thralls house was completely inadequate to house a growing community. The bishop placed his proposal before the council, who could not help but agree to it. Not only did the bishop feel the sisters needed a new convent, but he also was prepared to contribute five hundred dollars toward it, promising to match the gift upon his return from a trip to Europe in the spring of 1851 to procure more funds and priests for the diocese. His departure would last sixteen months, and in his absence Father John Corbe was appointed the vicar general and administrator of the congregation.

As the sisters celebrated their good fortune, Guérin was considering retirement. After years of poor health and the stress of guiding a growing community, she felt it would be better to have a younger, stronger person in charge, despite the fact that the bishop had appointed her the congregation's superior for life. She talked of returning to Ruillé to prepare for death. "I, who have not a fourth of your duties, am often quite overwhelmed by mine. Each day I become more broken down, more incapable, and also more lazy, and yet for me also the work increases while the strength diminishes," she wrote Mother Mary Lecor in July 1851. Despite her fatigue, however, Guérin began the Herculean project of constructing the new motherhouse. Although the congregation would incur a great deal of debt, she did not worry too much about the expense initially. Realizing the importance of the project, the bishop offered to help fund the project from the proceeds of the Vincennes mission for four years, contributing about twelve hundred dollars annually toward the building. In addition to the already promised one thousand dollars, the bishop contributed approximately six thousand dollars toward the building. Guérin signed the first contract with the quarry before September, and by September 18 the first load of stone for the building arrived.

However, while the bishop made good on his word to help finance the structure, the academy faced a decline in enrollment. In December Guérin wrote to Bishop Bouvier lamenting that "Our

The Academy of Saint Mary-of-the-Woods

schools have suffered much this year from Protestant opposition. There are now only thirty-three pupils at the Academy. Moreover, several of the Catholics do not pay. We are as poor as Job. It is impossible to think of building." She explained that she had used some of the bishop's money for daily provisions, which were once again scarce.

Thankfully the winter was a mild one, and Guérin and the workmen continued planning the building throughout the year and into the summer. The building was to be a three-story structure with a basement that would keep the building cool in the summer and guard against frost in the winter.

Guérin had a lot of misgivings about building the new house. There were moments when her resolve failed her, especially when money was tight. "We are beginning to build a house which will cost more than fifty thousand francs, a terrible undertaking for little persons like us. I feel my courage slipping away at the thought," she wrote. Privately she worried that there would not be enough students to justify incurring such a debt and prayed that somehow the school would get fifty students. On February 22, 1852, she learned that fifty-one students were registered. In light of this bounty of pupils, she was more committed than ever to the new building.

Throughout the spring and summer construction moved along on the new convent; however, delays were inevitable. The stifling heat of the summer months plagued the workers, who were firing bricks and having to accommodate rain storms that destroyed trees and caused a great deal of damage in the region. "Then there came a large swarm of locusts," Guérin wrote, "which made terrible ravages in our orchards. . . . Then they die, after having deposited, one knows not where, the seed for another generation."

By October 1852 work on the exterior of the motherhouse was nearing completion. Each day the sisters saw changes in the building as the walls rose higher. Just before November, the roof was nearly completed, and the sisters began to settle in for the last winter in their cabin.

When the bishop announced his return to America after stopping in Brittany to organize a group of postulants, or new sisters in training, he asked Guérin to travel to New York to help bring the women to the Indiana mission. For the first time since 1843, she traveled eastward and she noted that many changes had occurred in the region. Cincinnati was home to a new cathedral, and there was an increase in the number of Catholic churches she saw along the way. It was quite a change from her previous journeys when there were few Catholics in the region.

On arrival in New York, Guérin was blessed to learn that one of the new postulants was none other than Sister Saint Francis

Xavier's sister, Elvire le Fer de la Motte. "Elvire is a daughter made to order. I consider her a gift from the Lord, and if He spares her, she will do much good here," wrote Guérin. An ecstatic Sister Saint Francis Xavier wrote to Mother Mary, exclaiming, "At last I have seen and embraced her. My mother, I did not recognize her countenance, but how soon I recognized her heart . . . the Sisters all think her charming, and old Sister Olympiade has become ten years younger. I am afraid we shall spoil the dear child. . . . Thank you, thank you, my mother, for having consented to send us your treasure."

The bishop was pleased to discover that it would not be long before the sisters would be able to move into their new dwelling. As each new phase of the building was completed, Guérin shared the news of the accomplishments with her friends in the diocese and

New Providence Convent built by Mother Theodore in 1853

in France, reporting on each glorious detail as it unfolded, from the new chapel to the cross that adorned the building. She told her community back in Ruillé that the new chapel was the prettiest she had seen since coming to America and that the motherhouse was elegantly simple in its appointments. When she received word that Bishop Bouvier was sending a portrait of himself to the congregation, Guérin could hardly contain her excitement about the building, even though the sisters still owed approximately twenty to twenty-five thousand francs on the construction. "When you sent six of your daughters to Saint Mary of-the-Woods, you thought they were going to lay the foundation of an establishment which, later on, would be of service to religion . . . you never expected to see the fruits of your zeal crowned with so much success," she wrote.

Guérin found the house to be too much like a castle and not what a community of sisters should be used to and felt a little guilty knowing that the house could have been built less expensively and without as much finery. Afraid that her pride in the building might rub off the wrong way on her congregation, she wrote, "How unhappy I should be if, through my example, extravagance would be introduced among us." In fact, the house was a well-crafted structure that was very plain and without any modern conveniences. Everything was of good quality but simple in nature, with candles and oil lamps providing light and a few stoves and some small fireplaces for heat.

As the last doors were hung and the finishing touches placed on the beautiful gray and dark green building, the sisters' new home was blessed by Bishop Saint-Palais and Father Corbe on August 7, 1854.

M I C H I G A N

Chicago

Lac Michigan

Notre-Dame
South Bend

St. Joseph R.

Fort Wayne

Maumee R.

St Mary's R.

Tippecanoe R.

Logansport
Peru

Wabash

I N D I A N A

I L L I N O I S

O H I O

North Arm

St Mary-of-the-Woods

Terre Haute

Indianapolis

White River

Columbus

Montgomery
(St Peter's)

East Fork

North Madison
Madison

Vincennes

Jasper

Jeffersonville

ETABLISSEMENTS
ouverts par
Mère Théodore Guérin
(1840 - 1855)

St Francisville

New Albany
Lanesville

Louisville

St Meinrad

Wabash

Evansville

Ohio

K E N T U C K Y

Map of establishments and schools, 1856

Chapter 8

A Mother's Love

To say that Mother Theodore Guérin was committed to the education of young women at her various establishments is an understatement. After the new convent was completed, Saint Mary-of-the-Woods once again experienced significant growth. By early 1854 the Sisters of Providence had the responsibility of educating more than one thousand students, eighty-five of them at the academy alone. Other than the Franciscan Sisters of Oldenburg, the Sisters of Providence were the only congregation of women religious dedicated to the education of young women in Indiana.

Some of Guérin's success can be credited to the increased economic prosperity in Indiana. Years before, families could ill afford even partial tuition at Saint Mary's, but now more and more parents wanted their children educated by the sisters. Often entire families were represented at the academy as young girls followed their older sisters as soon as they were old enough. It was not uncommon for cousins to join them as well. This increased interest facilitated the need for building improvements and additions even before the new motherhouse was completed.

In October 1853 Sister Saint Francis Xavier le Fer de la Motte wrote to France, telling the superiors that the school was doing well primarily due to the sisters' efforts and the quality of the young girls in attendance. "Our boarding school has never been so flourishing. . . . Our Sisters are very zealous for the salvation of their pupils and have the consolation of counting among them some exemplary young girls." The result of this effort was ten converts in a single year. However, the reputation of the school was impeccable even among the Protestants. Guérin wrote Bishop Jean-Baptiste Bouvier of Le Mans, saying that "In America I have nowhere seen such care for the education of the pupils as is taken at Saint Mary's."

While Guérin remained humble about her contributions to the academy, it is clear that her involvement helped those around her feel confident and secure about their mission. She also had a very capable staff. Sister Mary Cecilia Bailly, her first assistant, was a constant source of intelligence as well as being a fine educator. Sister Maurice served as the community's scientific and artistic genius, Sister Saint Urban served as philosophy instructor, and Sister Mary Eudoxie Marshall was the head of the music department.

Despite the hard-earned reputation of the sisters, Guérin and the others still experienced waves of intolerance and bigotry, especially from Know-Nothings, members of an anti-Catholic movement. "They swear by the most frightful oaths. . . . Murder, deceit and all the horrors at which an honest soul trembles are the means they promise to employ and which they swear to practice at the peril of their lives. In one of the Indiana newspapers, they wrote that I am a tyrant, an abominable monster who keeps young girls against their will in our house, which they call a tavern or haunt of brigands," wrote Guérin. "For several days we thought they were going to come and burn us alive."

Public school legislation also did all it could to work against the schools established by the Sisters of Providence. Once the state set aside funds for a public school system, Protestants withdrew from the Catholic schools in record numbers. At first, many within the Catholic Church disregarded the anti-Catholic movement. Anti-Catholic sentiments were fueled by printed stories of novices being held captive by their convents. Such inflammatory articles made the public look twice at the sisters they had put such faith in not long before. "This is the first time this has occurred," Guérin wrote. Even visits by the bishop were used as an excuse for riots. At one point, Archbishop Cajetan Bedini, a visiting prelate, narrowly escaped being assassinated in Cincinnati.

SISTERS OF PROVIDENCE

Father Hippolite DuPontavice

Although Know-Nothings and other anti-Catholic and anti-immigrant groups created a dangerous atmosphere for American Catholics, it would take more than a few political waves to wreak havoc in the Indiana Catholic community. Father Hippolite DuPontavice of Madison wrote that the period showed the faithful what they were made of. "Nothing has ever proved the strength of Catholicism like the Know-Nothing movement. Nothing ever did so much good to our Catholics. The cold have grown warm again, and the tepid have become fervent. All united like one man round their Mother [the Catholic Church] when they saw her attacked. I am of the opinion that public thanksgiving should be offered to these K[now-] N[othings]. . . . I had much trouble in the parish for two or three years. . . . Now all is finished. . . . I have never seen so much piety, so much union around their poor pastor as today."

Guérin not only had the job of creating new establishments and working with her superiors to help foster the education of young people all over the state, but she also had to be the spiritual leader to those in her congregation. As her sisters wrote to her from their various missions, Guérin ministered to their needs, offering advice and a mother's love. For those at the motherhouse at Saint Mary-of-the-Woods, Guérin conducted daily instruction, teaching the sisters about the virtues of the Sisters of Providence. The instructions often centered on the Rule, personal spirituality, and how to be effective teachers. She likened the sisters' instruction of the children to that of Jesus who surrounded himself with little ones.

If she was the community's spiritual mother, there was little doubt that Jesus was its father. Guérin encouraged the sisters to turn to Jesus in times of crisis, as he never abandoned them. "He shares our miserable dwelling with us," she said. "He remains with us day and night. Yes, while you are peacefully sleeping, Jesus is watching over you. . . . He continues to exercise the same vigilance over us that he showed for his apostles."

Letters were the only means of communication among those who lived outside of Saint Mary's, and delivery was often slow. In those precious letters the sisters in the distant missions conveyed their problems, achievements, and news to Guérin. Sister Mary Xavier Lerée wrote from the orphanage in Vincennes about her difficulty controlling her temper with the children and her concern that she was withdrawing from the sisters with whom she was living. Guérin wrote to Sister Mary Xavier reminding her how much she loved her and offered her some advice for dealing with the children: "Remember that you have not only to teach them how to sew, but also how to become meek, humble, patient, etc. . . . be obedient, and above all, be patient. Never show temper with the children; but if you should do so, try to make amends by greater sweetness and condensation towards those poor little girls, who are not only children, but children bereft of their mothers," Guérin wrote.

Sister Maria Vicaire, living in Madison, often had feelings of self-doubt. In one of her letters, Guérin addressed Sister Maria's fear that she may be losing her mind, encouraging her through gentle chiding, to stop concerning herself with personal issues and to concentrate more on God. "My poor child, it would be better for you to be obedient than to be guided by your own poor judgment," Guérin wrote. "Repent of your sins and failings; take resolutions to do better and, after that, be quiet. The more we stir up a dung-hill the more it exhales bad odors."

The love Guérin had for the sisters was evident in her letters, as she constantly reminded the women how much she loved and missed them. She encouraged them to spread that same kind of love to the children they were ministering to and to demonstrate that love to everyone with whom they had contact. She even expressed this love to those women she had not yet met and who were due to arrive from France, writing to three postulants who were still at Ruillé and giving them a blunt account of life in Indiana and what they could expect from their travels to the Midwest. She encouraged them to think very seriously about their travels while there was still time to change their minds. "If your hearts waver, if you are afraid of the cross, of poverty, of humiliations, do not leave France; you would not be suitable for our little Community," she wrote to Nathalie and Justine Hermann and Mary Marshall. "If, on the contrary, you are determined to belong entirely to God, to endeavor by His grace to become humble, pious, and above all, to renounce your own will by obedience, then come. . . . He will bring you to our beloved Woods, where you will find Sisters who love you even now and who are praying for you. You will also find in your new country souls who do not love, who do not know God; but these whom you will instruct and direct in His service will be your crown in eternity."

Guérin's health was fragile long before she came to America, thanks largely to a bout of smallpox that she had during her novitiate, and she grew accustomed to continuous bouts of illness throughout the difficult Indiana winters. By the age of fifty-five, she had grown increasingly frail. Her strength was ebbing and she had difficulty walking. Again, she thought of retirement, but she always pushed those thoughts aside. "I consider these thoughts a temptation," she said. Thoughts of her health were of little consequence when there were needs of others to be considered.

The winter of 1854 was brutal, with unusually low temperatures that killed several of the community's animals. Once again, Guérin hovered near death with illness that winter. Although her recovery was gradual, when she learned of an outbreak of smallpox in Terre Haute, she personally went across the river to vaccinate children. Eventually she was able to tour her missions, where there was a remarkable amount of progress in Madison, Fort Wayne, Terre Haute, Evansville, and Jasper. The only establishment not growing was Vincennes, where enrollment had dwindled ever since the school was blended with the orphanage.

By the time Guérin returned to the motherhouse in June, a wet spring had turned into an unbearably hot summer. Food prices skyrocketed, and a lack of rain caused crops to wilt and die. Reports suggested that the conditions were the worst they had been in eighty years, and they continued to worsen through the fall. Writing to France, Guérin told Bishop Bouvier about the economic problems crop prices were causing in the area. "We have sort of a famine in the United States. . . . All provisions are expensive as gold. Potatoes are sold at an exorbitant price at New Orleans; everything else is dear in proportion. The wheat and potatoes failed entirely this year on account of the drought and excessive heat we have had to suffer this summer which is also considered the cause of the terrible maladies which under different names have decimated the United States."

Guérin was not the only one experiencing difficulty under the deplorable conditions. Father DuPontavice wrote the superiors in France about the sufferings of the Catholics in Indiana and Kentucky. Even Bishop Jacques M. Maurice Landes d'Aussac de Saint-Palais was having a tough time supporting two orphanages and a seminary. Luckily, generosity knew no bounds, and many rallied to support those who needed it the most. "There is great suffering on account of the food scarcity and hard times . . . but Providence is so good," Father DuPontavice wrote. "Money is scarce here, yet the collection for the orphans will be almost doubled. Vincennes alone gave more than eight hundred dollars for these poor children," Father DuPontavice continued.

As though agricultural problems and an economic downturn were not enough, the establishment at Terre Haute was the victim of another fire that summer. The fire started in the forest not far from the buildings at Saint Mary's. When Guérin saw it, she immediately gathered the workmen and the sisters into a fire brigade. Sister Saint Francis Xavier, who was in poor health, contributed by praying near the tabernacle. For over an hour, the group worked diligently to drive back the flames. Once it began to grow dark, they realized that the fire was not quite as fierce. As the teams came together to account for everyone, they realized that Guérin was not among them. She had last been seen by Sister Mary Eudoxie Marshall heading beyond the forest. As the group searched the woods, rain began to fall. Sister Saint Francis Xavier's prayers seemed to have worked.

Finally one of the workers thought he heard a faint voice in the distance and realized it was Guérin. When Guérin saw that the fire was dying, she had gone to the farmhouse to get a lantern and lost her way on her return. She had been sitting on a log for forty-five minutes and was prepared to sit there all night if necessary. As the group returned home, the rain continued to fall, putting out the remainder of the flames.

On September 12, 1854, Guérin traveled to Lanesville, a small village in southern Indiana between Corydon and New Albany, to start yet another school. Many German Catholics had settled in the area, and a small frame church and rectory sat on a parcel of land about six miles north of the Ohio River. The community's one hundred and twenty families and their pastor Father Alphonse Munschina were thrilled to welcome Guérin and the sisters. The new school was responsible for the education of sixty students, all under the age of twelve. Because the need for education was so great, many parents wept for joy with appreciation for the sisters.

After leaving Lanesville, Guérin and Sister Basilide Sénéschal left for Madison by steamboat. Their steamboat was supposed to arrive at night, but they were not notified of their stop. The two sisters had no choice but to continue to the next stop and try to catch the next boat back to Madison. They boarded the next steamboat and were heading down river when they were informed that the steamboat would not stop at Madison. The captain took pity on the sisters' plight and offered to have the sisters transfer from the steamboat to a small boat that would land them in Madison. The sisters were stepping into the small boat when a man jumped into it, pushing the boat away from the sisters, who fell into the swollen river. All Sister Basilide could do was watch as Guérin was up to her neck in water. More than once she worried that Guérin would lose her grip on the steamboat and succumb to the river.

Finally the small boat was steady once again, and it was able to row back and save her. When Guérin and Sister Basilide arrived in Madison, they were taken to the convent, where Guérin was examined for signs of pneumonia. Although Guérin was suffering from exposure and shock, she continued her journey to Saint Mary-of-the-Woods. After she arrived, she did not mention the mishap. None of the sisters knew what had happened until Sister Basilide returned to the motherhouse the following summer for the annual retreat.

Even in light of the accident, Guérin kept going. Nevertheless, it was obvious at least to Sister Mary Cecilia Bailly (later Mother Mary Cecilia) that the accident had a lasting impression on Guérin, and there were some affairs of the house she was no longer able to attend to. Years later, Sister Mary Cecilia noted that "every year we saw her weaker and more ailing . . . she would probably have lived several years longer bearing up against a suffering body but still managing the affairs of the Community . . . but for the accident on the river . . . she came home worse than usual . . . from this date, Mother's poor health sensibly changed for much worse."

In addition to her own physical difficulties, Guérin learned in February 1855 that her longtime friend and confidant Bishop Bouvier had died on December 29, 1854. He had traveled to Rome in order to hear Pope Pius IX announce the proclamation that the Blessed Virgin's conception was indeed pure and immaculate (Immaculate Conception). He had been ill on the journey but became worse after the proclamation and eventually died. Guérin took the death of the bishop hard. She had always looked to his guidance, love, and support and knew that he was due partial credit for the success of the community.

In her letter circular to the sisters dated February 10, 1855, she expressed how important Bishop Bouvier had been to the congregation over the years. "Our Community is indebted to him for its Rules and Constitutions. Saint Mary-of-the-Woods owes to him its very existence and preservation. This saintly and learned prelate was for us in our days of darkness what the cloud was for the Israelites in the desert—a shelter and a light. In our days of peace he was ever a father. Five weeks before starting on his great and last journey, he sent us his portrait, expressing his regret at not being able to come himself to his 'beloved daughters of the Woods.'"

Though it is unclear how many in the community realized that 1855 would be Guérin's final year, certainly several of them saw how weak she was becoming. Each month was a struggle, yet she remained committed to her duties. Many of the students and sisters caught heavy colds, and Guérin always seemed to be stricken more severely. During the preparations for the feast of Saint Joseph, Guérin came down with pneumonia. "I feel that I am becoming much weaker," she wrote to France in March 1855. "Since last June I have had a cough that gives me no respite, never leaves me. I have just had an attack of inflammation of the lungs which has weakened them still more, and further my voice is gone. . . . If God wishes me to die, I am resigned though it would cost me much to leave our Sisters."

As spring arrived, Guérin was not renewed as she had been in the past with the warmer weather. Sister Basilide anxiously awaited her visit to Madison, which had been delayed several times due to Guérin's health. Though Guérin chronicled in her diary that she was still unwell, Bishop Saint-Palais encouraged her to travel on the yearly visitation to the establishments. Accompanied by Sister Mary Joseph le Fer de la Motte, she left Saint Mary's on May 3. Despite Guérin's positive outlook on the journey, the trip was physically demanding and she took to coughing every time she talked.

"The trip did not do her any good," wrote Mother Mary Cecilia after Guérin died. "She came home somewhat worse than when she had left. She was so long ailing at the last place that she visited that she could not return by the same way she had come. She could not stand the hard and tedious travel."

Guérin made the trip to Madison, partially because she knew Sister Josephine Monaghan was very ill, and she wanted to be with her when she died. Health issues aside, she insisted on keeping up with correspondence and telling the community of its latest loss. "Our Lord has again plucked a flower from his garden at St. Mary's," she wrote in the letter circular to the congregation on May 20, taking the time to point out the virtues of Sister Josephine. "Her faith was immoveable, her confidence in God unbounded, her love for her Beloved, most ardent and strong. Oh! what a happiness it was for her to be permitted to take her vows, and with what fervor she pronounced them!"

As her health continued to fail, Guérin's letters became shorter and her diary entries brief. "We leave with the Bishop for Vincennes. I cough all the time and go to consult the doctor," she wrote on June 13. Although she was becoming a shadow of the woman she once was, she took comfort in the fact that the sisters and children were saying special prayers for her speedy recovery.

Many of the sisters saw Guérin as a woman who had returned from the brink many times, and so they waited for the recovery they felt sure would be forthcoming. Guérin knew otherwise. In July she wrote to Mother Mary Lecor in France and expressed to her the difficult conditions from which she was suffering. "This year God has given me a share in His cross, but I ought to tell you, dear Mother that I have never borne it so badly. To my ordinary ailments there has been added an affection of the chest which, for more than a year has caused me to suffer much and since the first of March has not left me a moment's repose. . . . I wished to visit the establishments. . . . Arrived at Fort Wayne in the month of May, I was two weeks in bed and scarce able to do a thing. Returning to Saint Mary's in much pain, though traveling by railroad, I have continued to be very sick."

Guérin's letter circular dated July 5 invited the sisters to their retreat. She longed to be part of the annual event, but her doctor ordered her to rest. With the bishop officiating and Father John Corbe serving as the retreat master, eleven novices were professed, six postulants received the habit, and four sisters took perpetual vows. Sister Mary Cecilia took Guérin's place at the retreat.

Guérin seemed to be hanging in a balance between life and death. On August 14 she was struck with malaria, making her medical situation worse. Guérin poured her heart out to Mother Mary in Ruillé, telling her some of her fears as well as her realization that the community would go on without her. "I neither die nor live. One week I am a little better and the next I relapse. . . . You can see now, dear Mother, that our Lord wished to make me see the truth of what you told me—that I was very proud and foolish to think that my Sisters still had need of me, as everything passed off perfectly without my having a hand in it at all. I do not doubt it will be the same when I shall have closed my eyes. I have said so to myself many times, but I did not know it so clearly as after the experience I had."

By September Guérin was feeling a little better, and she began another project. She wanted to construct a monument that would stand as a tribute to the Blessed Virgin, a large task for her to undertake given her condition. She already had several thousand dollars put aside for the new building, and she was determined to realize this dream. She wanted the chapel to be based on the plans for the church being built in Ruillé, so she wrote to Mother Mary requesting a copy of the plans. "You know, Mother, that we would like to build a chapel. We should have to be our own architect and surveyor. We entreat you then, dear Mother to send us the plan of your church, or, if you think it would not be suitable in our Woods, would you have the kindness to have one made by the person who made yours or by someone else?" she wrote.

Guérin was confident that this project was right for the community, as all of her debts were paid and things were going well for the sisters. Guérin planned for the chapel to be in Gothic style and one hundred feet in each direction. Ultimately, the building would not be completed until 1886 and was built in Italian Renaissance style featuring a lacelike tower. It is the church that graces the Saint Mary-of-the-Woods campus to this day. The

Interior of the Church of the Immaculate Conception, 1940

project seemed to give her a renewed sense of vitality, something that was noted by her physicians. Doctor John Isadore Baty came to Saint Mary's and found her heart stronger than ever. However, due to the coming winter, work on the project would have to be put on hold until the spring.

Although she was making numerous plans throughout the fall, Guérin did not have any delusions about her health. Writing to Sister Gabriella Moore in Fort Wayne, she made her condition quite clear. "You are in error if you think I am cured. I am far from it," she wrote. "But the One who has kept me alive until this day can continue to do so, if He so wills. He will not take me away until He no longer wishes to use this poor instrument anymore."

She continued to do well and was able to conduct business around the establishment. The sisters saw her around the convent just as they used to years before. In some ways it was like the old days. The year also marked the fifteenth anniversary of the Sisters of Providence in Indiana, and tremendous changes had been made in the time that the sisters had lived on Indiana soil. Not only had their own community grown to include sixty sisters, but they were responsible for the education of more than twelve hundred children across the state. While commemorating their time in the Midwest, Guérin did not hesitate to tell the sisters that there was still more work to do. On October 22, 1855, Guérin wrote, "What good is being done by the sisters of Saint Mary's! What good remains for them to do, if they are faithful to their holy vocation!"

That winter Sister Saint Francis Xavier fell ill as well with a raging fever and delirium. In the days leading up to Sister Saint Francis Xavier's death, Guérin wrote of her disorientation. "She thought herself cured," Guérin wrote. "On the 28th of January, sixth day of her illness, she had me called to confide to me the secret of her cure . . . her sister, Sister Mary Joseph [le Fer de la Motte], believed it, Sister Olympiade [Boyer] also; but I . . . who found her pulse 130, cannot tell you what I suffered in not being able to share my fears with anyone."

By January 31, 1856, the battle was near an end. Sister Saint Francis Xavier had her last few moments of anguish with Guérin at her side. Guérin took the loss hard, calling her the soul of the congregation. In her announcement to the sisters, a grief-stricken Guérin wrote, "You do not expect me, my dear daughters, to write a eulogy of her whom we have so many reasons to regret, of her whose absence leaves such a void in the Community. Her name alone suffices to bring to mind all that is sweetest, purest, and most attractive in virtue. She was for those who knew her the ideal of religious perfection. Not only have we unanimously considered her the saint of our Congregation, but persons of the world, even those of a different faith, could not behold her angelic exterior without being led to the thought of God."

Guérin's health once again became the public sign of her suffering. She maintained her correspondence with the sisters, and she asked Sister Mary Cecilia to come to the motherhouse to act as her assistant and guide for the novitiate. Knowing her time was growing short, she worried about her successor. She had written to Mother Mary in July 1855 about her guilt at not having the foresight to think about who would take over when the time came. "If I only had, as you say, a person to replace me. But there is none, and I do not know where to find one to train her. All these considerations have thrown me into a deep sadness. . . . You will blame me, no doubt, for not having provided against this contingency sooner. I blame myself; yet it seems to me that I could not do anything about it."

She didn't know where to begin to find a sister capable to take her place and she knew there wasn't enough time to train her successor. She considered the possibility of Sister Saint Vincent Ferrer Gagé or Sister Basilide but they didn't seem to be up to

1850

March.17/ I am obliged to keep my bed, what a beautiful week week to be upon the Cross. Beyond Cross, I will love *attaimer* the with all my heart...

A transcription of Mother Theodore's last words, diary entry for March 17, 1856

63

First convent cemetery

the task and she didn't feel that Sister Mary Cecilia was up to the challenge of governing a congregation despite having many of the qualifications one would like in a good leader. Privately, she hoped that Sister Mary Joseph would become the next general superior.

Holy Week marks the most solemn time in the church year, and Palm Sunday, March 16, 1856, was no exception. As the sisters gathered together for the Holy Week retreat, Guérin attended Mass but fell ill during the ceremony and had to leave. Somehow she knew it was to be her last celebration, and in her last diary entry she mused that it was a "beautiful week to be on the cross." Her condition grew complicated and conditions of the lung, heart, and digestive tract coupled with headaches and fever kept her confined to bed.

Physicians were called in but were cautious about placing a time line on Guérin's life. They had been wrong so many times before that they did not dare predict how long she would live. On Easter Sunday, as she suffered in bed, Guérin asked Sister Mary Joseph to write to the sisters at Ruillé and inform them that she was dying united in mind and heart with the community she loved so much.

True to form, Guérin felt better the Monday following Easter and asked to see the plan for the chapel that had arrived from France. She liked the design but felt that the building was too small. She discussed the location of the project with Father Corbe, who suggested that the chapel be constructed "as a wing to new Providence extending into the garden."

Her condition seemed to improve and worsen during the weeks that followed, and the sisters experienced a roller coaster of emotions as their hopes were raised and dashed for the recovery of their foundress. Those who wished to be near her were not turned away, and prayers were offered day and night throughout the community. Her beloved sisters ministered to her at her bedside, as well. Sister Mary Cecilia wrote that Guérin had "prepared herself long since. . . . The sacrifice of her life was made, her act of resignation perfected, and she received the notification with composure and calmly prepared herself for that moment, the most solemn for a Christian. . . . The room was full of weeping sisters, and an impressive silence prevailed, rendering more audible the words of the sad ceremony. No one dared to disturb the sacred solemnity by . . . outward demonstrations of grief, and strange to say, we still clung to the hope that, as it had happened before, she might yet recover."

On May 14, 1856, Guérin's fifty-seven-year journey came to an end at 3:15 a.m. after receiving prayers and absolution by Father Corbe. She was surrounded by her sisters, many who slept fully clothed in order to be near when the moment came. Sister Mary Joseph wrote to their friends in France saying, "This cherished Mother departed from her desolate daughters, from this land of exile, to enter on the road to her true country . . . a willing exile from her beautiful country, full of zeal for the salvation of her fellow beings, the charms of her mind drew them towards her, while the goodness of her heart attracted them to her."

Guérin was buried the next day, with Bishop Saint-Palais officiating. The sisters carried her to the cemetery on the knoll of Saint Anne, placing her remains next to Sister Saint Francis Xavier.

Sister Mary Joseph le Fer de la Motte

Chapter 9

Sister Mary Theodosia
Mug's Miracle

After Mother Theodore Guérin's death, Sister Mary Cecilia Bailly was named general superior to the congregation. Although Guérin had wanted Sister Mary Joseph le Fer de la Motte to replace her, she knew that Sister Mary Joseph did not have enough experience for the job and that Sister Mary Cecilia was probably the most qualified candidate, having served as Guérin's assistant for several years. It must have been hard to follow in the footsteps of such a pioneering spirit, but Mother Mary Cecilia did not shirk her responsibilities and quickly made tremendous contributions to the community.

A little over twenty years after the Sisters of Providence at Saint Mary-of-the-Woods was founded, the country was ripped apart by the Civil War. Indiana governor Oliver P. Morton was a strong supporter of President Abraham Lincoln, even though the state was divided when it came to public opinion about the war. After the April 12, 1861, attack on Fort Sumter, the tide changed, and Morton quickly sprang into action.

With fifty-three thousand Indiana men invested in the war, it was important to Morton that they were cared for properly and in appropriate medical facilities with trained personnel in place. City Hospital (present-day Wishard Memorial Hospital) in Indianapolis was turned over to the federal government for the care of the soldiers wounded in battle. At the time, a limited number of trained nurses were available. This critical need inspired some to consider using women religious as nurses, providing them with rudimentary medical training. The Sisters of Providence had some medical expertise because their Rule stated that they must have an operating pharmacy at their establishments. Realizing they were excellent candidates, Morton approached Father Augustine Bessonies, the pastor of Saint John Catholic Church in Indianapolis, for his assistance in enlisting the help of the sisters. Mother

Gravestone of Sister Athanasius Margaret Fogarty, a "U.S. Army Nurse Civil War"

Mary Cecilia immediately traveled to Indianapolis to see what needed to be done. The Sisters of Providence took charge of the hospital's administration on May 17, 1861.

The Nuns of the Battlefield *Civil War monument*

The sisters were in charge of all domestic tasks, such as washing, cooking, and cleaning. One of the first tasks they were given was to sanitize the bedding used by the wounded, thoroughly cleaning every mattress and room. After being cleansed and dressed in clean clothes, the soldiers were placed in beds where they could begin to recover from their wounds. Many of the sisters also served as nurses, risking their lives to the infectious diseases of the time, including typhoid, dysentery, and measles. Eleven sisters served, and their graves bear the inscription "U.S. Army Nurse Civil War." One of them was Sister Athanasius Margaret Fogarty, who served as the director of the hospital as well as Saint John's Infirmary, a rehabilitation facility for soldiers, which closed in 1871.

The sisters' efforts were well respected and recognized to the point that the Sisters of Providence are represented on a national memorial in Washington, DC, for the contributions made by several religious congregations. The monument is titled *The Nuns of the Battlefield*. Their efforts are also honored at the Colonel Eli Lilly Civil War Museum in the basement of the Soldiers and Sailors Monument in Indianapolis.

In addition, the sisters kept up with their educational establishments, beginning with the rebuilding of the original academy in 1860. Over the years, all of the various superiors made contri-

138

Mother Mary Ephrem Glenn

Mother Euphrasie Hinkle

SISTERS OF PROVIDENCE (2)

butions to the legacy of the congregation. Mother Mary Ephrem Glenn (1874–83) was the first superior to establish missions beyond Indiana, and she greatly reduced the debt the sisters incurred during the panic of 1873, when the country was in financial turmoil. Mother Euphrasie Hinkle (1883–89), who converted from Methodism, established the first mission in Chicago, as well as the first Sisters of Providence mission on the coast in Chelsea, Massachusetts. She was also in charge of the construction of the Church of the Immaculate Conception, Guérin's last major project.

The diocese also changed during this time. In 1857 the northern part of the state was renamed the Diocese of Fort Wayne, and after the bishop of Vincennes began living in Indianapolis in 1878, the name of the diocese was changed to the Diocese of Indianapolis on March 28, 1898. It would be elevated to an archdiocese in 1944 with the inclusion of two Suffragan Sees: the Diocese of Evansville and the Diocese of Lafayette.

There were those within the diocese and elsewhere who did not forget Guérin or her legacy. Many people remembered the kind French sister with dark brown eyes and a fair complexion. It is not surprising that many considered her to be a saint or to have those qualities associated with saints, but it was not until 1909 that the official Cause, or campaign for canonization, was begun.

The process toward canonization in the Roman Catholic Church is long and thorough and requires intense investigation of a person's life along with evidence of two miracles that occurred as the result of the person's intercession with God. During the early years of the church, "a reputation for a holy life, a great spirit of charity and a report of miracles was the only requirement for sainthood." During the Middle Ages, however, simply being popular was not enough of a reason to be declared a saint. By 1234 there seemed to be a need to create formal procedures for canonization, beginning with the local bishops. Pope Gregory IX engineered the procedural norms that guide investigations into a person's reputation for sanctity. The Congregation for the Causes of Saints office was established in Rome to help oversee the Causes that were introduced by the various bishops throughout the world. A core group (people seeking a canonization) appoints a postulator, which means "one who asks." This person is trained in canon (church) law and is approved by the office of the Congregation for the Causes of Saints and acts as a liaison between the Vatican and the core group.

Despite reports in recent years of a fast track to sainthood, Pope Benedict XVI has said that modern men and women need true models of holiness and that saints need to be chosen with care.

Francis Silas Chatard, bishop of Indianapolis

SISTERS OF PROVIDENCE

The pope also stressed that there should be a real "fame of holiness" surrounding a candidate for sainthood, not just the conviction of a small group that the person led a good Christian life. The canonization of a saint is not the creation of a demigod. Rather, it is a way to honor those deceased men and women who have proven to possess heroic virtue and can serve as role models to people everywhere. While there are prayers associated with saints, they are intercessory prayers asking a saint to pray for a person rather than prayers of worship.

Guérin's Cause technically began in 1907, when her remains were exhumed and moved from the Sisters of Providence cemetery to the crypt in the Church of the Immaculate Conception. Bishop Francis Silas Chatard of the Diocese of Indianapolis inspected the body and discovered that Guérin's brain had not decomposed despite being buried for fifty-one years. Bishop Chatard, a physician who had graduated from the University of Maryland Medical School in 1854, knew that this was an unusual event. He immediately requested that three other physicians be brought in to examine his findings. Prudently, he also requested that one of those doctors be a non-Catholic in order to better verify this phenomenon. This proved to be the first physical sign that Guérin was worthy of closer examination, and it was indicative to all of those involved in the process that there was something unusual about this woman's life. According to one of the doctors who investigated the remains, the discovery was highly unusual since "the brain is the most delicate tissue in the human body and normally it disintegrates within six hours after death."

After the medical reports came in, Bishop Chatard formally opened the Cause in 1909. The first step in the path to sainthood is the informative process. During this phase, the bishop investigates a candidate's life, sifting through any writings by the individual or pertaining to him or her. The bishop also collects testimony from those who knew and worked with the individual in question. All information that is collected is transmitted to the Vatican by the bishop.

During the informative phase of Guérin's Cause, twenty-four individuals offered personal accounts of their experiences with Guérin. Among them was Father John Corbe. As chaplain at Saint Mary-of-the-Woods he had spent much time working with her and helping her through some of her darkest times. In his personal account he wrote of the moments he spent with Guérin just after she died: "I had never seen her so beautiful, and in the midst of my sorrow and of that desolating scene, I could not cease to contemplate her with a secret consolation. She did not seem to me to be dead, but to be sleeping in the sweetest and most peaceful sleep. It is thus that the saints die, or rather, that they sleep in the Lord at the end of their beautiful lives filled with good works and virtues."

Léon Aubineau, a journalist from France, met and interviewed Guérin during her fund-raising trip to Europe. Although his experience with her was quite limited, he was affected by her spirit, stating, "No one knew her without loving her, and no one spoke to her without carrying away an ineffable remembrance . . . we saw her only once . . . we are still, as on that first day, under the spell of that exquisite eloquence."

Mother Anastasie Brown

142

Sister Mary Eudoxie Marshall, like Father Corbe, had a much closer relationship with Guérin. At the age of twenty-three, Marshall lived with her mother in the convent of Ruillé as a "parlor boarder," or tenant. Proficient in French, Latin, and music, she answered the call when she heard that Bishop Jacques M. Maurice Landes d'Aussac de Saint-Palais needed sisters to travel to America and help with the Indiana missions. She spent four months in the novitiate before making her journey to America, where she ultimately became the head of the music department at Saint Mary-of-the-Woods. She also translated all of Guérin's letters and journals. At the age of eighty, she testified for the Cause, saying, "She [Mother Theodore] observed her vows perfectly. I know this from personal observation. She practiced all the virtues in a high degree. . . . She was always occupied and never permitted others to lose time. She was just in all her dealings."

Another witness, Mother Anastasie Brown, knew Guérin both as a student at the academy and as a sister within the community. She was the first student from the academy to enter the novitiate, and in time she served on the Sisters of Providence council with Guérin. In 1868 she became the third superior general of the congregation and the first Ameri-can-born woman to hold that prestigious office. Writing on behalf of Guérin's legacy, she said, "she did everything for the glory of God. She had a firm faith that did not turn aside . . . her faith remained firm until her death, and I have often heard her repeat in her instructions that she was ready to give her life for her faith."

Mother Mary Cleophas Foley

143

In 1908, while Bishop Chatard was still collecting testimony, an incident occurred that sent Guérin's Cause into high gear. Sister Mary Theodosia Mug was born in 1860 in Attica, Indiana. Her mother was Ellen Phillips Mug, a former academy student who received instruction for First Communion from Guérin in the 1850s. Sister Mary Theodosia was also a student at the academy, spending time with many of the sisters who worked with Guérin. She graduated in 1877 and joined the order the following January, eventually becoming a teacher.

Like Guérin, Sister Mary Theodosia had her share of health problems. As a young woman, she was afflicted with neuritis, a painful condition caused by the inflammation of the nerves, in her right hand and arm. By 1902 she could no longer teach due to the pain. Although Sister Mary Theodosia traveled to Michigan for treatments in hopes of making her condition better, the neuritis recurred. She also discovered that she had developed an abdominal tumor, which Doctor Leon J. Willien of Terre Haute confirmed, but chose not to operate on or remove it.

In addition to her teaching, Sister Mary Theodosia was a gifted writer. She spent time with some of the founding sisters of the community, interviewing them and writing down their recollected memories of Guérin. In 1900 Bishop Chatard asked Mother Mary Cleophas Foley to assign someone to the task of writing a biography of Guérin. She called on Sister Mary Theodosia, and the result was *The Life and Life Work of Mother Theodore Guérin, Foundress of the Sisters of Providence at Saint Mary-of-the-Woods, Indiana*. It was published in 1904.

Because of Sister Mary Theodosia's condition, writing was a laborious task. Since she could not lift her arm, she had to write her manuscript by hand using a pencil and balancing the paper at knee height. Nevertheless, she did not let her afflictions get in the way of her love for writing. She not only wrote the biography, but also a book on the Civil War efforts of the sisters titled *Lest We Forget: The Sisters of Providence at Saint Mary-of-the-Woods in Civil War Service*, which was published in 1931. She also edited Guérin's letters and journals, published in 1937.

In 1906 Sister Mary Theodosia discovered that in addition to her other health problems, she had a cancerous tumor in her left breast. Doctor Willien proposed an immediate surgery in order to spare her life. The ensuing radical mastectomy was crude by today's standards. Although the one tumor was removed, the surgery left damaged nerves on her left side, and as a result, her left arm hung rigid at her side and was completely useless. Doctor Willien chose not to operate on the abdominal tumor because he feared it would be more than Sister Mary Theodosia could handle.

Despite the surgery, the sister's cancer was not gone. In fact, it was growing. Her health was in a precarious state and seemed to be deteriorating quickly. She was plagued by continuous vomiting, and the abdominal tumor became so large that she could not sit comfortably and was only able to kneel and walk with great difficulty. In spite of her troubles, she continued to work—writing and editing.

Sisters in the convent routinely went into the depths of the church to pray near the crypts of the sisters whose remains were kept in the vaults. On October 30, 1908, Sister Mary Theodosia went to the crypt in order to pray for the health of an ill sister. Standing near the crypt of Guérin, she wondered if Guérin had any power with God. "Instantly, I heard in my soul the words, 'yes, she has,'" she wrote in her account of this incident to Mother Mary Cleophas. "I was so startled by the suddenness and distinctness of the words— not any external voice or sound but an utterance to my soul." Sister Mary Theodosia moved quickly away from the crypt, fearing that if she stayed, she might actually see whatever or whomever had just spoken to her. "I paused and chided myself for my excitement—I am never afraid of the dead; why should I fear now?"

Reflecting on the words she had heard, Sister Mary Theodosia remarked that if Guérin had this power, she sure wished she would use it. After that, she went on about her evening, working late into the night and determined to put the incident out of her mind. Still, as she worked with her printing, proofreading, and writing, she thought of the words she had heard hours before.

She awoke the next morning feeling, in her words, "strong and rested." She could not believe that she had been in bed for only three hours. Without thinking, she made her bed, and as she spread her coverlet, she noticed she was using both of her arms.

Before, making the bed had been a considerable effort for her, as she could use only her right arm. "For the first time since February 3d, 1907, I rolled up my hair without resting my head on my knees. With suppleness, strength had returned, the fingers being as strong and quick on the piano, typewriter, etc., as if I had kept in daily practice," she wrote.

Sister Mary Theodosia Mug

Sister Mary Theodosia also discovered that the waistband of her clothing was too large and that the tumor below her waist had diminished. The painful lump that had prevented the sister from genuflecting and walking normally had disappeared. "What became of the lump, I do not know, but I feel nothing abnormal since that day. Moreover, I see now as I never saw before, and the exactions of setting and reading type seem never to cause a moment's fatigue to the eyes."

Her stomach and digestive issues also had been resolved to the point where she could eat every kind of food imaginable. She wrote that she could "eat anything that comes to the table, and in such quantities as to amaze everyone. . . . I had been the worst kind of dyspeptic, dieting always and for long periods able to take no solid food whatever . . . it is truly most wonderful."

In the following months, medical professionals examined Sister Mary Theodosia, but no one found any trace of her malignancy. When people commented on the radical change in her condition, she had only one explanation: "Mother Theodore cured me." The cancer never returned, and she died of old age on March 23, 1943, at the age of eighty-two.

At the time of Guérin's death, a person had to be deceased for at least fifty years before a Cause could be presented for consideration. Recent developments have allowed Causes to be introduced five years after a person has died, although that time line has been waived for Mother Teresa of Calcutta and Pope John Paul II. When Guérin's Cause was opened a year after Sister Mary Theodosia's healing, it was just a little more than fifty years after her death.

World politics also placed a great deal of strain on how many saints could be canonized at all in the twentieth century. Not long after the informative phase of Guérin's Cause was completed, the country was hurled into World War I, which saw many American men travel overseas only to be among the millions who died in the European trenches. In the brief peace that followed, Guérin's writings were approved on July 25, 1927, by Pope Pius XI, which means that the Vatican felt that her writings were consistent with the way she reportedly lived her life. Ten years later, the dioceses of Saint Briuec and Le Mans in France were studied and people were interviewed, since Guérin had ministered and lived there as well. Unfortunately, World War II halted the Cause before the cardinals at the Vatican could vote to continue it. The cardinals did so on December 6, 1955.

Everything that had happened up to this point was considered to be part of the diocesan phase of the Cause. In addition to having testimony from those people who actually knew the candidate and having any and all writings analyzed, the bishop has to ensure also that the candidate does not have any kind of "cult-like" following that may run contrary to the rules of the church. The results from the bishop's investigation of Guérin, both in Indiana and in Europe, were compiled to form the Acts of the Diocesan Cause for Canonization. While the original copy of the acts was kept in the archives of the diocese, two authenticated copies were sent to Rome. One would be kept in the archives of the Congregation for the Causes of Saints and the other would be available to those who were to compose the *Positio*, or documented account of the life, work, and writings of a holy person such as Guérin.

Two months after the cardinals voted to continue the Cause, Pope Pius XII approved and signed the petition opening the Apostolic Process for the Cause. During this process, the Congregation for the Causes of Saints examines all documents pertaining to the candidate in order to verify that the candidate as well as any document dealing with the candidate is conducive to the norms of the church. Once approved, an appointed official and an assistant, often the postulator, work together to create the *Positio*. In the case of Guérin, that duty fell to Sister Joseph Eleanor Ryan, who traveled to Rome in 1978.

A *Positio* is made up of two parts: the *Informatio* and the *Summarium*. The *Informatio* presents a great deal of detail about the life and virtue of the candidate, while the *Summarium* summarizes the deposition and testimonies of witnesses on key issues during the diocese investigation. It is aimed to demonstrate that the candidate, especially when he or she is not a martyr, lived a life of Christian charity not only to God but also to his or her neighbor and that his or her daily actions were practiced in a heroic manner. In 1988 the *Positio* had enough information to sufficiently judge the sanctity of Guérin and was officially approved on February 15,

1992. The following July, Pope John Paul II bestowed the title of "venerable" on Guérin as a person who lived a virtuous life to a heroic degree.

In the meantime, as early as the 1950s rumors surfaced of a miracle regarding the 1908 healing of Sister Mary Theodosia. Although many years had passed since the alleged miracle took place, meetings were held from November 5, 1956, to October 20, 1958, at Saint Mary-of-the-Woods and in Indianapolis. A panel led by Archbishop Paul C. Schulte heard from twenty-eight witnesses, including six clergymen, thirteen Sisters of Providence at Saint Mary-of-the-Woods, and nine laypeople.

In the canonization process, miracles are not used to simply show that the candidate is powerful or that the candidate has influence over God. Rather, miracles are a way for those involved with the canonization process to prove that the candidate is in heaven and able to assist the living. If a candidate is declared to be a martyr, or someone who dies for his or her faith, then miracles are not required for canonization. It is believed that those who die as martyrs go straight to heaven.

Alleged miracles are put through a rigorous testing process. Some of the miracles that have been reported over the years include healings and incorruptibility, where the saint's body has not decayed after death. In the case of Saint Catherine of Siena, her body has still not decayed although she died in 1380. Liquefaction is another phenomenon where the dried blood of the saint liquefies every year on the anniversary of his or her death, and the odor of sanctity is when the body gives off a sweet aroma. Other events that have happened during a person's lifetime might be considered miraculous and help move a cause for canonization along. They include levitation, where the saint floats in the air; the presence of the stigmata, or the five wounds of Christ, which usually bleed during Mass; and bilocation, where the saint reportedly appears in two places at once.

Healings are one of the most popular miracles to be investigated. When an alleged miracle is presented, a number of medical, scientific, and theological experts come together to scrutinize the event, searching for alternative explanations. If they cannot find another reason for the incident occurring, they report that to the church. The experts themselves do not have the power to declare the episode a miracle.

Even though the healing of Sister Mary Theodosia did not pass medical scrutiny until 1996, the *Positio* was presented to the Special Commission of the Congregation of Saints on February 5, 1992. In part, the *Positio* reads: "Mother's piety showed itself by her love of religion, her spirit of prayer, especially her application to mental prayer, and by her zeal for the exercises of devotion authorized by the Church. Her piety led her to study [spirituality]; in which she was well versed . . . she knew religion so well . . . religious instruction was her favorite occupation. . . . Here was that piety which is a gift of the Holy Spirit which sanctifies and proves itself by marks of visible progress on the highway of Christian perfection."

The Statement of Heroic Virtues of the *Positio* was reviewed by a panel of eight theological consultants who offered written opinions of the life Guérin lived and her prospects as a saint in the Catholic Church. One consultant believed that Guérin lived a life of heroic faith through the acceptance of the great adversities that she had to endure. A second consultant said that Guérin's diaries and letters served not only as an autobiographical sketch of the woman, but also as an insight to her very soul.

Another consultant recognized that Guérin's Cause faced a lengthy and arduous process, not because there was any doubt of her holiness, but rather there were "extrinsic" difficulties in addition to a lack of personnel "capable of conducting a canonical trial." The consultants also stated that Guérin "can be considered a pillar of the American evangelization . . . in Mother Guérin we single out a soul who chooses to seek sanctity while drawing others along the same path of perfection."

After a unanimous affirmative vote on the *Positio*, John Paul II beatified Guérin on October 25, 1998. In his statement, the pope said that Guérin was a "holy woman of God [and] lived a life of extraordinary love. Her love for God totally filled her being. . . . Her love embraced even those who caused her pain and anguish. She transformed the hardest hearts by her inspired words. . . . In her words, 'Put

Sister Diane Ris

yourself gently into the hands of Providence,' she recognized that all she did was in God's loving care. . . . This woman, Mother Theodore Guérin, is indeed a woman for our time. She is a model of the best of womanhood."

The sisters at Saint Mary-of-the-Woods received the news from Sister Diane Ris, who was the general superior of the congregation at the time. She and over one hundred other sisters, along with Archbishop Daniel M. Buechlein, three Indiana bishops, and other devotees from both Indiana and France, traveled to Rome to be part of the festivities. During the ceremony, Sister Joan Slobig and Sister Margaret Ann McNamara, general officers of the congregation, presented a plaque to the pope. The plaque was made from a tree at Saint Mary's and included an inscription taken in part from the pope's remarks. The plaque stated, "We must break open the cycles of despair in which are imprisoned all those that lack decent food, shelter or employment. . . . On the occasion of the beatification of

Mother Theodore Guérin, our Foundress, we, the Sisters of Providence of St. Mary-of-the-Woods, Indiana, recall the generosity of the pioneer family of Saint Mary of the Woods who offered housing to Mother Theodore and her five companions when they reached the dense forests of Indiana in 1840 only to find themselves homeless." As a gift offered on the occasion of Guérin's beatification, the Sisters of Providence established a revolving loan fund to help make adequate housing available in West Terre Haute.

Sister Angela Garlat, who was ninety at the time of the beatification and retired from teaching, celebrated the announcement at the Church of the Immaculate Conception with the other sisters. Speaking with a reporter, she said she was very happy about the beatification and that she was grateful to be part of the celebration. "This woman who labored only 16 years in the place called St. Mary-of-the-Woods has packed this church today and has caused over 400 pilgrims from all over the world to descend on Rome to sing her praises. It is amazing. It is awesome. It touches a deep place in one's soul," Sister Nancy Nolan commented.

But the process was not complete. For the sisters and all of Guérin's supporters there were still more hurdles before their beloved foundress could be declared a saint. As Sister Marie Kevin Tighe, the vice postulator for the cause, stated, "one more stamp of approval by God, one more inexplicable intervention in the laws of nature" was required before Guérin could be declared a saint in the eyes of the church.

The vice postulator worked diligently on the Cause and sorted through a constant stream of mail from those who claimed that favors were granted as a result of Guérin's intercession. Looking for that one case that might lead to the final steps toward canonization, Sister Marie Kevin said that the crux of the cause was not in the miracles. "What is really significant is how Blessed Mother Theodore lived her Christian religious life. . . . Mother

Theodore's life was characterized by a profound faith and trust in God's loving Providence. She believed that God loves and cares deeply for each person and that, as Sisters of Providence, she and all of her sisters were to make God's Providence known and experienced through their works of love, mercy and justice among God's people."

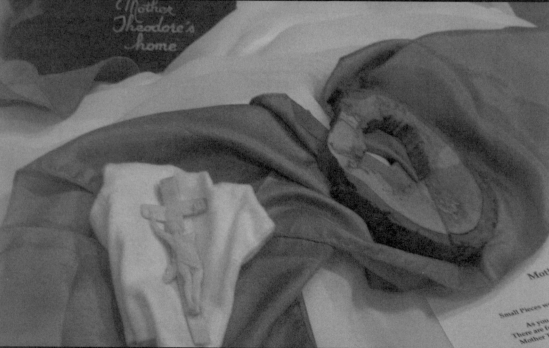

The Rosary (top) and Cross (bottom) of Mother Theodore Guérin are displayed as part of a makeshift shrine honoring Guérin in Rome.

Chapter 10

Saint Theodora Guérin

Since 1996 Sister Marie Kevin Tighe has served as the promoter of Mother Theodore Guérin's Cause for canonization, but between 2002 and 2006 she has also acted as the vice postulator for the Cause. Much of her time has been spent answering letters and reporting on favors granted through Guérin's intercession as well as meeting with travelers who come to Saint Mary-of-the-Woods to see the place that Guérin founded in 1840. A popular stop on the tour is Providence Center, where visitors can view some of Guérin's personal items that are on display in the Heritage Room. Sister Marie Kevin also travels, speaking to a variety of groups about Guérin's legacy as well as updating people on the canonization process.

Sister Marie Kevin was not at all surprised that Guérin's Cause took ninety-seven years to complete. As it turned out, the last fourteen years of the Cause saw more progress than the previous eighty-three. The progress is largely due to relatively stable global affairs and having a postulator on the Cause, who must be a resident of Rome, who was committed to staying with it until the very end. According to Sister Marie Kevin, "The postulator in a Cause for canonization is an intermediary between the requesting group, in this case, the Sisters of Providence and the Office for the Congregation of Saints in Rome."

However, over the course of the years there have been ten postulators, all of whom had to leave the post for one reason or another. One man became a bishop and was transferred, while another lasted a couple of years before becoming ill and dying. As each new postulator was appointed, time was lost as each had to become familiar with the Cause and the vast amount of documents involved. "We had to do that ten times before Mother Theodore was declared 'venerable,'" said Sister Marie Kevin. "That first step is the hardest because Rome has to see that everything that was written by and about the person is consistent with the church's teachings," Sister Marie Kevin continued.

Not only was the changing of postulators a problem, the Cause was slowed down by two world wars, the Great Depression, and the second Vatican Council. While Vatican II was an important process for the church, it was time-consuming and caused the progress of the Cause to stall. Once the title of "venerable" was bestowed upon Guérin, the sisters realized that they needed a postulator who would stay the course for the duration of the Cause.

The sisters hired Doctor Andrea Ambrosi, a layman, who had worked within the Congregation for the Causes of Saints for over thirty years, had studied canon and civil law and several languages, and had a desire to serve as a postulator. Ambrosi began to review

Rita Ambrosi, Andrea Ambrosi, and Sister Denise Wilkinson

157

the files on the Cause, one of which contained the testimony referring to the 1909 cure of Sister Mary Theodosia Mug. Initially, the case had seemed questionable to one person, but upon closer inspection, Ambrosi "had a different reaction and was especially impressed with the extreme rapidity of the cure." This, coupled with the Sisters of Providence community's tenacity in continuing to promote the Cause, was his motivation for advancing the Cause.

After Sister Mary Theodosia's cure was accepted as the first miracle and the title of "Blessed" was bestowed on Guérin in 1998, Sister Marie Kevin began the investigation for another miracle. Several cases were worth noting. One case involved a woman in Joliet, Illinois, who was suffering from macular degeneration. Her daughter, a former student at Saint Mary-of-the-Woods College, had given her a third-class relic of Guérin's, a small piece of linen touched to the bone of the foundress. According to Sister Marie Kevin, the woman prayed with the relic every day. During a visit to her doctor, the physician noted that her eyes had improved and asked what she had done. She told him that she prayed. A case in Boston involved a man who was suffering from throat cancer. He and four generations of his family had been educated by the Sisters of Providence. At one of his doctor visits, the oncologist inquired, "Now where did that thing [tumor] go?" To this day the man remains cancer free and believes that the cause of his recovery is due to Guérin's intercession.

Although neither of these cases went to a formal trial, Sister Marie Kevin took notes on them as well as any other e-mail or letter that arrived that would promote the Cause or lead toward canonization. Little did she know that the miracle she was looking for was closer to home than she realized. In fact, it was brewing right under her nose.

Phil McCord was not expecting a miracle. Brought up Baptist, he had been employed as the director of facilities management for the Sisters of Providence since 1997. Even though he worked for a religious community, he did not consider himself to be a praying man. Although McCord suffered from eye problems since childhood, by the time he moved to Terre Haute he was afflicted with cataracts, myopia, and astigmatism. McCord's left eye was worse than his right, so doctors postponed surgery on his eyes until the right eye caught up with the left. The first operation took place on September 21, 2000, and was a success, with McCord experiencing better color awareness and light perception. His peripheral vision also improved.

However, a few months later McCord underwent a second surgery for a cataract in his right eye. Following the surgery, he felt a "heaviness" around the eye and could not see out of it. He also experienced a drooping eyelid and a pulled, reddened face. McCord and his physician hoped that with continued treatment, his condition would improve. However, it did not, and the surgeon sent him to a specialist in Indianapolis. The specialist confirmed that his cornea was swollen and he would need a cornea transplant. The procedure had a 60 percent success rate and required more than two years of recovery time, not to mention countless risks, including blindness. "To say that it [weighed] heavily on my mind would be an understatement. I just kind of moped around for a couple of weeks, thinking about it. And I finally got to the point where I just didn't think I could do it," McCord said.

One day, as McCord walked down a hallway next to the Church of the Immaculate Conception, he heard the sound of a pipe organ. He entered the church, settled into a pew, and looked around at the various statues, religious icons, and frescos that graced the walls of the church. He decided to pray for the strength to overcome his fear about the surgery. "I try to do things myself," he said in a silent prayer. "But that's not going to happen this time. I'm not going to be able to do this. Can you help me deal with this problem? Can you give me some strength?"

Phil McCord

159

In the midst of this prayer, he thought about Guérin. He remembered the sisters' belief that she had intercessory power with God and wondered if she might be able to help him. He prayed, asking her to help this humble servant. Then he stopped, questioning what he had said. Are you a servant if you are a paid employee? After debating the issue for a while, he finally decided to drop the pomp and circumstance and just spoke from the heart. "Mother Theodore, if you have any influence with God, I would appreciate it if you would exercise it on my behalf and kind of help look out for me," he prayed. McCord felt better for having turned his problem over to God, and he returned to work. Even though his sight was not any better, he felt calmer about the situation and began to think that perhaps he could get through the surgery.

The following day his vision was still unclear, but the heaviness around his eye was gone and he felt different. When he went to the eye specialist for a follow-up appointment and to schedule a date for the surgery, he told the doctor that he was feeling much better. "It was kind of funny," McCord reported. "He looked at my eye . . . and looked back at my chart, and he said 'hmmmm.'"

The eye specialist asked him if his surgeon had done anything to the eye, to which McCord said no. The doctor then asked him if he had done anything to the eye to account for its improvement. McCord responded that he had prayed. "So I asked him, 'Well, do we wait now for a while to schedule the surgery for later?'" McCord said. "He said, 'No, you don't need the surgery.' I was stunned to say the least." Once the swelling went down, McCord's condition was further improved through a laser treatment. He has perfect vision, although he still uses reading glasses when he needs them.

According to the *Indianapolis Star*, medical experts have differing opinions on what might have happened. McCord's ophthalmologist in Terre Haute, Doctor Jeffery A. Jungers, could not explain the recovery, but hesitated to rule it as a miracle. Doctor Nicholas Rader, a Catholic and a Greenwood ophthalmologist who reviewed the case at the church's request, said that the incident was not only inexplicable, but it was also a miracle. "For me, the whole thing came down to 'Why did it happen right after he prayed?'" said Rader. "There are certainly causes and conditions that could have been present all along that might have improved the condition, but when they asked me, my final answer was 'As a scientist, I have no explanation, but as a Catholic I do.'"

McCord shared his story with one of the sisters, who casually mentioned that it sounded like a miracle. McCord agreed, but little did he know that this word choice would propel him into a whole new realm of inquiry. "I didn't know it had happened until one of the sisters came and said, 'Did Phil tell you about his eyes?'" Sister Marie Kevin said. "I said 'no' so I called him and he came over and it sounded pretty solid and so we began communicating with the postulator [Ambrosi] and started with the process of investigating it. Even though we had the other case in Boston, the postulator told us we were only going to work one case at a time."

Investigations into miracles are time consuming and expensive to conduct; therefore, each one that is looked at must be chosen with care. There are two trials to the process: the informal and formal trial. For the informal trial Ambrosi came from Rome in 2001 and met with McCord, his wife, and the surgeon. Ambrosi was convinced of the case's merit and recommended moving on to a formal trial, which encompassed 150 questions from Rome. Sister Marie Kevin was instructed to find eight witnesses and two doctors who had nothing to do with the case to examine McCord as well as look over the medical records. Each of the witnesses testified at the Metropolitan Tribunal of the Archdiocese of Indianapolis, which was presided over by two priests, a notary, and another doctor. "They were very scientific in their line of questioning," said Rader.

One by one the witnesses testified between January and April 2003. A doctor who was not one of the two who examined McCord offered to transcribe the fifty-five pages of medical records. After transcribing each note made by the doctors, the physician offered to be one of the witnesses. "The postulator was surprised at that and said that it was rare when a doctor wanted to be one of the witnesses," said Sister Marie Kevin. By June 2005 the five-person medical commission declared that the healing could not be explained by medical science.

In November the seven-person theological commission appointed by the Congregation for the Causes of Saints in Rome began looking at the case. "I'm not a theologian. I don't understand all of the implications of what happened to me or how they determine it to be a miracle," McCord said. "I just leave it to those who are more learned in that area. All I know is that it is my story and I am sticking to it."

Monsignor Frederick Easton, vicar judicial for the Archdiocese of Indianapolis, said that the commission reviewed both the miracle and the acts of the Cause and decided there was nothing contrary to faith or morals in the miracle and life of Guérin. The next step toward sainthood was a vote taken during a regular meeting of the Congregation for the Causes of Saints. All that was left afterward was for the pope to approve the Cause and then a formal date for canonization would be set.

As Sister Marie Kevin waited for each piece of news that told her the Cause was moving forward, Teresa Clark was commissioned by the Sisters of Providence to begin work on a statue of Guérin to be displayed at the National Shrine of the Immaculate Conception in Washington, DC. Clark began her work in the spring of 2005, shaping eight hundred pounds of clay into Guérin's likeness.

In order to capture Guérin's spirit, Clark studied her life and worked with old illustrations of the sister. She created a small model before working on a six-foot clay model that was shipped to a stonecutter who carved a statue out of Indiana limestone for the national shrine. Clark's statue portrays Guérin as "a woman walking in stride, with her hand reaching out to show her as a woman of both action and compassion." "When you are thinking that intensely about someone and you are trying to create their face in the process, momentarily, it is almost like they are really there, or influencing or inspiring," Clark said.

As many of the sisters peeked in on Clark's work, several commented that it was like meeting Guérin for the first time. "I have seen some older sisters walk up to the statue and just have tears fall down their cheeks," Sister Marie Kevin said. "I've looked at pictures of Mother Theodore all of my life. But I never had the same feeling as I do when I look at the statue because it is more than a physical likeness. The statue exudes the spirituality of Mother Theodore, which is strength and peace and trust in God." Sister Marie Kevin said that she did not hear a single complaint about the rendering.

As the statue neared completion, the Sisters of Providence learned on February 21, 2006, that the cardinals of the Congregation for the Causes of the Saints had approved the findings of the McCord case and deemed it an authentic miracle. The way to canonization was now open. The sisters at Saint Mary-of-the-Woods celebrated their news with a press conference, where they introduced the world to McCord, whose case had been guarded carefully. Sister Ann Margaret O'Hara, the congregation's general superior, said, "I think it is a special day of joy because it celebrates the heritage of Mother Theodore and that is still alive in this place and that she came to this part of the world for the good people of this area."

McCord admitted that the healing had a profound impact on him, but he is quick to note that he is still not much of a churchgoer. At one point he even asked Sister Marie Kevin if his healing qualified as a "small thing." She replied that it was not a small thing to him and to accept it as an act of love, noting that Guérin had a great deal of affection for the workers at Saint Mary's. "She was right there with them working in the fields," Sister Marie Kevin said. "She had a great deal of respect for them."

As the case was handed over to the cardinals and bishops of the world for review, the sisters were busy preparing for the canonization and answering questions from the press, knowing that the fate of their foundress rested on the desk of Pope Benedict XVI. In the days that followed, the sisters began to make travel arrangements in order to accommodate anyone who wished to attend the canonization. Meetings were held to decide what name should be bestowed upon Guérin when she became a full-fledged saint. Some of the sisters were partial to Saint Anne-Thérèse, while others favored Saint Theodore. In the end it was decided that they would ask the pope to declare her Saint Mother Theodore Guérin.

Finally, at the beginning of May 2006, Benedict XVI agreed with the consensus that it was through the intercession of Guérin that McCord was healed. As he signed the decree acknowledging the miracle, the only thing left to do before declaring her a saint was to meet with the key cardinals who advise the pope on such matters. "We are very grateful for Pope Benedict's recognition," said Sister Ann Margaret. "Mother Theodore truly led an inspirational life devoted to God and to serving God's people." Sister Marie Kevin said that serving as the promoter for the Cause all of these years has been the "cherry on top of a wonderful life. I have always had a profound devotion to Mother Theodore [and promoting the Cause] has called me to a desire for a deeper expression of her virtues."

Benedict XVI's final approval came on July 1, 2006, when he announced that Guérin would be canonized on October 15, 2006, along with three others: Rafael Guizar Valencia, a Mexican bishop who was active in the Mexican Revolution tending the wounded and operating a secret seminary; Fillippo Smaldone, an Italian priest who founded an order of nuns known as the Congregation of the Salesian Sisters of the Sacred Hearts and promoted the education and assistance for the deaf; and Rosa Venerini, another Italian who established the Congregation of the Holy Venerini Teachers and also established some of the first public schools for girls in Italy.

The Sisters of Providence at Saint Mary-of-the-Woods were thrilled when the pope announced the date for the canonization, and while many celebrated the life and contributions that Guérin made, others prepared for the logistics of bringing more than five hundred people to the Vatican for at least three days of ceremonies. Outside of the Terre Haute community, Blessed Theodore Guerin Catholic High School in Noblesville made plans to purchase a permanent sign that would reflect the school's new name. As Sister Jeanne Hagelskamp worked at the new Providence Cristo Rey High School in Indianapolis, due to open in the fall of 2007, she remarked, "For me, it is a celebration of who she was and the values she espoused, her spirit of risk-taking and her unwavering Providence of God."

By the end of July, word of Indiana's first saint had reached the highest offices of Hoosier government. On July 21, 2006, Governor Mitch Daniels installed a portrait of Guérin on the south wall of his office in the statehouse, honoring her among other important Hoosiers. Flanked by several members of the Sisters of Providence, Daniels remarked that he felt good about being watched over by Guérin and stated that "She obviously came as near to perfection as a fallen human can, and as someone who is so tragically short of her standards, I think she ought to be up there for a long time." Monsignor Joseph Schaedel, vicar general

Governor Mitch Daniels and students hanging Mother Theodore's portrait in the statehouse

of the Archdiocese of Indianapolis, said having Guérin's portrait in the governor's office was a wonderful opportunity to show how religion played a large role in Indiana's earliest days as a state. He said there was a great spiritual connection between residents of the state and Guérin. "She is one of us," Schaedel said.

As the date for the canonization approached, the Vatican decided that Guérin's official name as a saint would be Saint Theodora Guérin. The reason for the name change was to give the Catholic Church one common name by which she would be known. The word "Mother" from her name was dropped in order to show that as a saint, her sanctity extended beyond the ministry she began at

Saint Mary-of-the-Woods. The Vatican permitted the Sisters of Providence to call her Saint Mother Theodore.

In accordance with Vatican law that states a saint's remains have to be kept in a prominent location, the Sisters of Providence removed Guérin's remains from the floor of the Church of the Immaculate Conception to the sanctuary of the church, allowing visitors to touch the simple coffin that contains her bones. Five hundred people were present on October 3, 2006, as six of the sisters wheeled in the coffin made from walnut trees grown on the Saint Mary-of-the-Woods property to the middle of the church. According to the *Indianapolis Star*, Sister Denise Wilkinson cried as she escorted the coffin through the church and throughout the service, saying that the sisters had waited a century to see the canonization of their foundress, who had not only served as their spiritual leader but also as a pioneer of Catholic education in Indiana.

Daniel M. Buechlein, the archbishop of Indianapolis, commented on Guérin's contributions for the education of young people as well as her indomitable spirit. "Her ability to persevere and remain loyal to a bishop who clearly had personal problems was a testimony to her character," Buechlein said. "She was a noble woman and a woman of very great integrity."

All eyes turned to Rome as the canonization drew near and more than 1,500 pilgrims from around the world celebrated Guérin's life with the Sisters of Providence in the 450-year-old Church of the Gesu in the heart of Rome on October 14, 2006. As members of the congregation recounted her life story, the sisters noted that "Laurent and Isabelle Guérin certainly did not know when their oldest child was born that someday she would merit the recognition of the universal church as a Saint of God." In the evening, members of the Saint Mary-of-the-Woods community as well as those of the community of Etables,

France, placed water from both Guérin's homeland as well as Saint Mary-of-the-Woods, her rosary, her white cross, a rock from Etables, and a letter that she wrote on a makeshift shrine honoring Guérin. Among the guests in the standing-room-only church were students from "Saint" Theodore Guerin High School in Noblesville and Guerin College Prep in River Grove, Illinois, alumnae from Saint Mary-of-the-Woods College, and descendants of the Thralls family. Anne Guérin and Martine Guérin Galant, relatives of Mother Theodore, were also present. Everyone in attendance had a story and a reason for wanting to be at the church to honor Guérin.

"After I started learning about her, she became more of a friend to me rather than just someone whose picture is on the wall of my school," said Deseriee Haines. Dan Thralls of Lafayette, Indiana, came to Rome to honor the woman that his ancestors worked alongside in 1840 during that first harsh Indiana winter. "It's nice to think you had family who were walking around with a saint," he said. "It's kind of humbling."

Finally, on a crisp sunny morning on October 15, Mother Theodore Guérin was canonized Saint Theodora Guérin as more than 50,000 people crowded into Saint Peter's Square. At least 1,200 of those people were Guérin supporters, including Sisters of Providence, students and graduates of the institutions Guérin founded, members of the Archdiocese of Indianapolis, and students from the newly renamed Saint Theodore Guerin High School. Concelebrants of the Mass included all five Indiana bishops and one from Guérin's homeland in France.

In a two-hour ceremony full of pomp and circumstance Guérin's supporters saw their years of hard work come to fruition. Waving blue scarves that were gifts from the Sisters of Providence, Guérin's fans, although outnumbered by the Italian and the Mexican communities, cheered mightily for Indiana's saint.

McCord carried the Sisters of Providence's gift to the pope along with Sister Marie Kevin and Sister Denise. The gift was a $5,000 check for helping women and children. "It didn't really hit me until I made that last turn and there the pope was with the basilica behind him," said McCord. "He was really in the moment and he didn't act like it was just another ritual. It was amazing."

During his homily Benedict XVI applauded Guérin's determination to leave all that she knew behind in France in order to carve out a life for herself and her sisters on the Indiana frontier. "'Go sell everything you own then, come, follow me.' These words have inspired countless Christians throughout the history of the Church to follow Christ in a life of radical poverty,

Sister Denise Wilkinson, Phil McCord, and Sister Marie Kevin Tighe present the gifts at the canonization Mass

trusting in Divine Providence. Among these generous disciples of Christ was a young Frenchwoman, who responded unreservedly to the call of the divine Teacher." The pope also spoke about the role faith played in Guérin's accomplishments. "With great trust in Divine Providence, Mother Theodore overcame many challenges and persevered in the work that the Lord had called her to do. By the time of her death in 1856, the sisters were running schools and orphanages throughout the State of Indiana. In her own words, 'How much good has been accomplished by the sisters of Saint Mary-of-the-Woods! How much more good they will be able to do if they remain faithful to their holy vocation.'"

Pope Benedict XVI

JULIE YOUNG

The pope gave his official blessing on the four newest saints, saying:

In honor of the Most Holy Trinity, with the lifting up of the Catholic faith and the creed of Christian life, by the authority of our Lord Jesus Christ, of the blessed apostles Peter and Paul and our own authority, with long reflection having taken place and having implored many times God's help as well as the help of our brothers' counsel, we today determine and find that Beatos (Blessed) Raphaelem Guizar Valencia, Philippum Smaldone, Rosam Venerini and Theodore Guérin are saints, and we inscribe them into the Catalogue of Saints of the universal church, and say that they must be remembered with pious devotion of all the saints. In the name of the father and of the son and of the Holy Spirit.

With these words Saint Theodora Guérin joined Saint Katherine Drexel, Saint Francis Xavier Cabrini, Saint John Neumann, Saint Elizabeth Ann Seton, Saint Rose Phillippine Duchesne, Saint Isaac Jogues, and Saint Rene Goupil as the eighth American saint and the first from Indiana.

Temporary shrine of Saint Theodora Guérin, Saint Mary-of-the-Woods

DAVID TURK

Learn More about Guérin

The Sisters of Providence at Saint Mary-of-the-Woods continue to work in the fields of education, health care, peace and justice, and eco-justice. More information regarding the history and ministries of the Sisters of Providence may be found on their Web site, http://www.spsmw.org/.

The girls' academy founded by the sisters in 1840 is now Saint Mary-of-the-Woods College. http://www.smwc.edu/.

Saint Theodora Guérin was a prolific writer, and her diaries, journals, and letters are in the archives of the Sisters of Providence of Saint Mary-of-the-Woods. A printed version of Guérin's writings, *Journals and Letters of Mother Theodore Guérin: Foundress of the Sisters of Providence of Saint Mary-of-the-Woods, Indiana* (Saint Mary-of-the-Woods, IN: Sisters of Providence, 2005), is the fourth printing of a volume that was first published in 1937.

Biographies of Guérin include: Katherine Burton, *Faith Is the Substance: The Life of Mother Theodore Guérin* (Saint Louis: Herder, 1959), Penny Blaker Mitchell, *Mother Theodore Guérin: A Woman for Our Time* (Saint Mary-of-the-Woods, IN: Sisters of Providence, 1998), and Penny Blaker Mitchell, *Mother Theodore Guérin: A Woman for All Time, a Saint of God* (Saint Mary-of-the-Woods, IN: Sisters of Providence, 2006). Sister Mary Borromeo Brown, *The History of the Sisters of Providence*, vol. 1 (New York: Benziger Brothers, 1949) details Guérin's founding of the order and establishment of schools in Indiana.

Information on the Catholic Church, saints, process of canonization, and other subjects can be found in *New Catholic Encyclopedia*, 2nd ed. (Detroit: Thompson and Gale, 2003) or online, http://www.newadvent.org/.

Archbishop Daniel M. Buechlein of Indianapolis wrote a series of articles on Bishop Simon Bruté, the first bishop of Vincennes, that in addition to biographical information on Bruté contain information on the early days of the diocese and the recruiting of priest and religious from Europe. The thirteen articles appeared in *The Criterion*, the archdiocesan newspaper, in the summer of 2005 and can be accessed online at http://www.archindy.org/brute/columns.html.

Information about the French Revolution and the Napoleonic era can be found at http://www.napoleonguide.com/.

A number of newspaper articles covered Guérin's Cause for canonization. These include the following:

Brandon Evans, "Cause for Canonization of Blessed Mother Theodore Guérin Moves Forward," *The Criterion*, June 24, 2005, and "Sainthood Cause of Blessed Mother Theodore Moves Forward," *The Criterion*, December 16, 2005.

Sean Gallagher, "'The Way Is Now Open': Blessed Mother Theodore Guérin Closer to Sainthood," *The Criterion*, March 3, 2006, "Employee's Healing Leads to Possible Canonization," *The Criterion*, March 3, 2006, and "A Work of Art, a Work of God: Artist Finds Faith in Sculpting Statue of Blessed Mother Theodore Guérin," *The Criterion*, April 28, 2006.

Robert King, "Following the Path Toward Sainthood," *Indianapolis Star*, April 29, 2006, and "Moving Closer to Sainthood," *Indianapolis Star*, May 3, 2006.

Guérin's path to sainthood can also be tracked through the Sisters of Providence Web site, http://www.spsmw.org/.

Banners of the four candidates for canonization hang in Saint Peter's Square. Saint Theodora Guérin is on the far right.

JULIE YOUNG

Index